early
Listening Skills

Diana Williams

Speechmark

DIANA WILLIAMS qualified as a speech and language therapist from the School for the Study of Disorders of Human Communication, London in 1983. Since qualifying she has worked for several years in schools and nurseries with children who have communication difficulties. She is co-author with Jackie Cooke of *Working with Children's Language*, which was first published by Winslow Press/Speechmark Publishing in 1985.

She has developed a specialist knowledge in the field of hearing loss and completed an MSc in speech therapy with deaf people at City University, London in 1992. Her research interests include the effectiveness of training programmes for education staff in the management of attention and listening difficulties.

Recently a lecturer in communication skills and communication disorders in children at the Central School of Speech and Drama, London, Diana is studying for a PhD, investigating the use of video analysis systems to evaluate communication skills. She is also working as a freelance lecturer.

> Please note that in this text 'she' is used to refer to the child for the sake of clarity alone.

Published by
Speechmark Publishing Ltd, Telford Road, Bicester, Oxon, OX26 4LQ
United Kingdom
Telephone: +44 (0) 1869 244 644   Fax: +44 (0) 1869 320 040
www.speechmark.net

© Diana Williams, 1995
Reprinted 1997, 1998, 1999, 2000, 2001, 2002, 2003, 2004, 2005, 2006

002-2604/Printed in the United Kingdom/1010

British Library Cataloguing in Publication Data
Williams, Diana
    Early listening skills
    I. Title II. Series
    428.3

ISBN-10: 0 86388 344 3
ISBN-13: 978 0 86388 344 6
(Previously published by Winslow Press Ltd under ISBN 0 86388 217 X)

EARLY LISTENING SKILLS
Contents

ACKNOWLEDGEMENTS

This book would not have been possible without the support and encouragement of friends and colleagues. I would particularly like to thank the following: former colleagues in the health and education services in Lewisham and Southwark; Jackie Cooke and Nina Gray-Lyons for their support for my work; Stephanie Martin for her advice and guidance; colleagues at the Central School of Speech and Drama for their support and assistance; and Annette Maczka and Sue Veasey for their help with details of the school curriculum.

Finally, I would like to express my appreciation to the children and families with whom I have worked and who have provided inspiration and motivation for this project.

INTRODUCTION

The ability to detect sound and attach meaning to it is the foundation block for the development of spoken language. From an early age children become aware of the sounds around them, especially the familiar voices of their parents and siblings. A variety of experiences help the children to extend this knowledge and learn to recognize sounds and understand speech. Listening skills become of paramount importance when the child enters the learning environment of the school, and are equally important to the child's social development as she attends to others and participates in conversations. The ability to attend to sound and to listen to spoken language is an integral part of the development of speech, language and communication. The sense of hearing also provides many hours of pleasure through listening to music, songs and stories, not to mention radio and television.

Many children with communication difficulties need to improve their listening skills. They may be delayed in their development of auditory skills or have difficulty in maintaining attention to auditory stimuli. Children with a hearing loss have an obvious disadvantage in developing these skills. Auditory information may be distorted or not audible to the child. Professionals, parents and carers intending to use these activities with deaf and hard of hearing children should always consult appropriate specialists such as audiologists, teachers of the deaf, and specialist speech and language therapists/clinicians (deafness).

Early Listening Skills is intended for use by professionals who are working with children who have underdeveloped listening skills, associated with language delay, hearing loss or another communication difficulty. The activities are designed to stimulate and develop auditory attention and auditory perceptual skills.

The majority of the auditory stimuli are non-speech sounds, although there is one section specifically on listening to spoken commands. Sounds and soundmakers range from notes played by musical instruments to everyday sounds in the home.

The activities are primarily aimed at the pre-school age group, but they can be modified to suit the needs of a range of children. For instance, older pupils at school can learn the vocabulary associated with sound and the sense of hearing.

HOW THE ACTIVITIES ARE ORGANIZED

Sections 1–10 of the manual cover auditory detection, discrimination, recognition, sequencing and memory. Additional sections describe holiday listening projects and topics for the school curriculum. A comprehensive list of sounds and soundmakers is given at the end of the book.

The early sections cover the basic auditory skills needed by the child before she can start to attach meaning to sound. Later sections deal with more advanced abilities, including sound recognition, auditory sequencing and listening to spoken commands.

Each section describes teaching activities that use a variety of soundmakers to develop the target listening skill. Activities sheets are provided with each teaching activity. They can be distributed to other professionals, parents or carers who may want to reinforce the child's learning. The activities on these sheets are aimed at helping the child to generalize the skills she has learnt in a structured setting to the home or school environment.

HOW TO USE THE ACTIVITIES

It is essential that activities are compatible with the child's auditory and language abilities. The introduction to each section will help the user to decide whether the child is ready for a particular stage, or needs less advanced activities. Some listening skills, such as sequencing activities and listening to speech, can be worked on simultaneously. Others follow a strict developmental sequence; for example, the child must be able to detect a sound before she can learn to recognize it. The choice of activities will also depend on the individual child. A profoundly deaf child may need specific teaching on sound detection before she is ready to try the activities in discovering sound and exploring soundmakers.

Teaching Activity

Most sections have several teaching activities. (Although these are for individual children, they can easily be adapted for groups.) These detailed activities will be particularly useful for students or professionals new to the area of language delay and hearing loss. They can also be used as training material.

Useful Words and Phrases

A list of words and phrases has been included alongside each teaching activity. This is intended only as a guideline which the user may choose to omit. It is possible to demonstrate the expected responses to the child non-verbally in many of the activities. Alternatively other words or phrases may be substituted which are more suited to the language and cultural needs of the individual child. The consistent use of instructions will provide structure and repetition of language.

Increasing the Complexity of the Activity

Advice is provided on how the complexity of each teaching activity can be increased. These suggestions can be used to adapt the activity to the needs of the individual child.

Variations

A list of variations is included with each teaching activity. It has suggestions for similar activities and ideas on how to vary the teaching activity to meet the child's interests. These have a variety of levels, so the adult needs to be aware of the child's overall capabilities when selecting alternative games. For example, an activity using picture material is developmentally more advanced for the child than one using large objects.

Activities Sheets for School or Nursery

Activities sheets for school or nursery accompany each teaching activity. The activities on these sheets are aimed at helping the child to generalize what she has learnt from structured activities to the school or nursery environment. They will also reinforce the child's learning of specific listening skills. The majority of the activities are for small groups or the whole class, with some suggestions for individual work.

One or more activities can be selected for the child. The following considerations should be borne in mind when selecting activities:

◆ the auditory, cognitive, linguistic and developmental needs of the child;

◆ the child's everyday routines;

◆ the child's educational curriculum;

◆ the child's interests, likes and dislikes;

◆ the availability of materials;

◆ the teacher or nursery officer's preference for activities.

These considerations should be discussed with the education staff, and activities explained and demonstrated if possible.

The activities sheets for school or nursery can be photocopied and given to teachers and nursery staff. Tick the selected activities in the box provided. For example:

 Team games

The children are divided into two teams, who take it in turns to find a ticking clock hidden in the room. Each team is timed to see which is the quicker to find the clock.

Activities Sheets for Parents

Activities sheets for use at home accompany each teaching activity. They provide practical advice on ways to use the child's everyday routines to learn about sound and games to develop the child's listening skills.

The majority of the activities are for one to one work with a parent or other family member. There are some suggestions for group activities which could be played as a party game or with the child's friends.

One or more activities can be selected for the child. The following considerations should be borne in mind when selecting activities:

◆ the auditory, cognitive, linguistic and developmental needs of the child;

◆ the child's everyday routines;

◆ the social and cultural context of the child;

◆ the child's interests, likes and dislikes;

◆ the availability of materials;

◆ the parent or carer's preference for activities.

These considerations should be discussed with the family, and activities explained and demonstrated if possible. The parent is not a teacher and therefore activities should avoid new or difficult skills for the child. The aim is for the family and child to enjoy the experience of listening together.

The activities sheets for parents can be photocopied and given to the child's family or carers. Tick the selected activities in the box provided. For example:

 'Blind Man's Buff'

One child is blindfolded. The other children move around. The blindfolded child tries to catch the other children by listening for any movements.

List of Suitable Materials

A list of suitable soundmakers, sounds, toys and other material is given for each target listening skill and sound source. These items have been selected as the most appropriate for the activities in a particular section. They include commercial products, standard educational equipment, everyday objects, toys, games and home-made items. The list can be photocopied and distributed to other professionals, parents and carers and should be used in conjunction with the corresponding activities sheet.

Advice should be given on the suitability of the equipment and materials for individual children. The child's cognitive, linguistic and developmental level will determine the choice of materials. (See 'Auditory Stimuli' and 'Materials for Teaching', below.) Sounds and soundmakers should be selected on their audibility to the child. Professionals, parents or carers should be consulted regarding the child's preferences and the availability of items. After discussion suitable items can be ticked. For example:

Materials for listening to animal names in simple commands:

Suggestions for toys and other items that can be used to represent animals are:

- ☑ photographs
- ☑ pictures from magazines
- ☐ line drawings
- ☐ *Plasticine* models
- ☐ papier-mâché models
- ☑ animal puppets

Checklists

The checklists provide the parent or professional with a way of recording the child's activities and her responses to sound. Information should be recorded about the sounds, soundmaker, target listening skill and the response of the child. One example is provided for guidance at the top of each checklist.

SETTING UP LEARNING SITUATIONS

Follow these guidelines to make optimum use of the learning situation:

1 Check that the child is comfortable and ready to participate.

2 Make sure she is seated in a way that allows her maximum involvement in the activity. She should be able to see, touch and hear equipment and be able to move around easily if required.

3 Reduce background noises and distractions so that the child can concentrate on the activity. If you are working in a classroom or a nursery try to have an uncluttered corner with plain walls that can be partitioned off. This is particularly important for children who have a sensory impairment and do not see or hear as well as they should.

4 Carry out the activities with an adult who is known and liked by the child. She is more likely to co-operate and enjoy the games. A familiar person will also be able to observe and interpret the child's responses.

5 Repeat the activities frequently. Constant repetition may be necessary to develop a child's skills. This is especially relevant for deaf and hard of hearing children who need a considerable amount of help in making sense of what they hear.

For group activities:

1 Decide how you will seat the children. Those children sitting in the middle of a semi-circle are in the best position to hear a speaker at the front. Also think about lighting – the hearing-impaired child needs to be able to see the speaker's face clearly.

2 Seat the children according to how well they work with other children and their own needs and preferences. An active child may attend better if she is seated between two quieter children. A passive child may sit still when at the outside of a semi-circle but needs adult help to make sure she participates.

PLANNING THE ACTIVITIES

Plan activities carefully before you start a programme of work. Use the following guidelines:

1. Choose activities that are appropriate for the child's auditory, cognitive and linguistic level. The activities should build on the child's strengths and help to improve her auditory abilities.

2. Use the guidelines on increasing the complexity of the activity to expand her skills.

3. Be clear about your aims for the child: always check the child's record of progress to see if they are appropriate for her needs. (See 'Monitoring the Child's Progress', below.)

4. Decide which sounds, soundmakers or words are appropriate to use in the activity. (Select these from the list given for each activity.)

5. Decide what responses you require from the child: this will depend on the type of activity and also on the abilities of the child. (See 'Responses from the Child', below.)

6. Use instructions that are clear, simple and within the language abilities of the child. The activities can be modified for children who have a limited understanding of spoken language. For example, the required responses can be modelled by the adult.

7. Plan how you will prompt the child if she needs help during the activity. Try the following cues:
   ◆ repetition of instructions or auditory stimuli;
   ◆ demonstration of the task by an adult or another, more able child;
   ◆ pointing, physical manipulation or gesture;
   ◆ removing choices so that the child does not have to make a decision.

8. Plan how you will praise the child and give feedback. If the child is to learn to attach meaning to sound, it is essential that she is aware when she has made an incorrect response. Avoid being too negative. Help the child to respond correctly by repeating the stimuli and prompting her.

9. Adapt the activity to suit the individual child's level of concentration. Children who have difficulties in listening often have short attention spans. The child's ability to concentrate will determine the length of the activity. The number of stimuli may also need to be reduced to help the child focus her attention.

10. To maintain the child's interest, use the suggested variations. The child can also become the leader in the activities.

AUDITORY STIMULI

Many children have difficulties with listening skills, but those who have a hearing loss are at a particular disadvantage. Sounds mat be distorted or inaudible to the child. Therefore it is very important to select auditory stimuli that are within the hearing range of these children.

A hearing-impaired child may have difficulty in hearing quiet sounds or sounds of a certain frequency. Generally loud sounds that are low in frequency are more suitable, but this is *not* the case for every child. Check your choice of sounds or soundmakers with the child's audiologist, teacher of the deaf or specialist speech and language therapist/clinician (deafness).

MATERIALS FOR TEACHING

Activities may require the use of a variety of equipment, materials and toys. These need to be selected with just as much care as the auditory stimuli. Remember:

1 A balance needs to be maintained between new and familiar material. Too many new things may frighten or bewilder a child, or overstimulate her so that she is unable to attend to the task; too many familiar items and she may become bored, making it difficult to maintain her interest.

2 Materials should be appropriate to the child's developmental, cognitive and linguistic level.

3 Toys and materials should be easy for the child to manipulate.

4 The child's interests, preferences and experiences should be taken into account when choosing materials.

5 Suitable materials are suggested at the beginning of each teaching activity. If these are not appropriate for the child, try the alternative materials listed for that teaching activity.

RESPONSES FROM THE CHILD

When planning activities you need to consider the responses the child is expected to make to the auditory stimuli and how the child will participate in the activity. Remember:

1 A child may give a variety of responses to auditory stimuli, including the following: eye or pupil widening; stilling; smiling or some other change in facial expression; turning to locate the sound; a change in vocalization (for example, quietening or increased sound production); reaching towards the sound; pointing; body movements (such as jerks); gesture or sign; and spoken language.

2 The activities require children to participate using a variety of means so that even those with limited vocal skills can take an active part by: eye-pointing, looking, touching, picking up a toy or picture, copying an action, copying a sound or word, vocalization or using speech.

Make it clear to the child how you expect her to participate in the activity by explaining or modelling the response.

3 Some responses are open to misinterpretation and you should look for patterns and consistencies before deciding whether a child is actually responding to sound in an activity.

Be aware of responses that indicate the child is confused or misunderstanding and modify the activity accordingly.

4 The desired responses should be within the range of the child's overall capabilities, not just her listening skills: for example, if a child is expected to turn and look for a sound, how good is her head control and sight? The other areas to consider are physical, visual, cognitive, linguistic and social skills.

MONITORING THE CHILD'S PROGRESS

1 Record information about the activities you carry out with the child. It is useful to note the following information:

◆ *Type of activity* – the area of listening skills being focused on, such as sound recognition.

◆ *Aims* – what you wanted to achieve with each child.

◆ *Description of the activity* – name of the activity or a brief description.

◆ *Equipment* – soundmakers and other materials used in the activity.

◆ *Organization of the activity* – individual or group session. Any special arrangements should be noted.

◆ *Expected responses* – what you are expecting from the children.

For example:

Type of activity Listening to speech, responding to commands with one information-carrying word. Using food vocabulary. Key words to include bread, milk, orange, biscuit, cake, banana.

Aims To improve attention to spoken language.

Description of the activity Shopping game – food laid out in a 'pretend' shop (table). Children asked to fetch items from shop by adult.

Equipment Real food items, plastic shopping bag.

Organization of the activity Group of four children.

Expected responses To select items of food by name without prompts, such as "Get me a banana."

2 Record what responses you *expected* the child to make and compare these with the child's *actual* responses in the activity. This information will help you decide if the activity is too easy or too difficult for the child.

Example of an individual record sheet:

Name of child	David
Expected response	To fetch single items when requested.
Actual response	David was able to fetch two items when requested.

Example of a group record sheet:

Expected response	To fetch single items when requested.

Name	Response
Gary	Able to select one item by name.
Meena	Able to select one item when name used with gesture.
Fatima	Able to select two items by name.

3 Make a note of the prompts and cues used by the adult to elicit the required response from the child. This information will also be useful in helping you to decide if the activity is too easy or too difficult for the child. The next stage may be to continue with the activity but gradually reduce the prompts and cues.

Example of an individual record sheet:

Name of child	Myra
Expected response	To fetch single items when requested.
Actual responses	Myra was able to fetch single items when gesture was used with word.

Example of a group record sheet:

Expected response	To fetch single items when requested.

Carl	/		/	
Toni			/	
Farouk				/
Cemal			/	

SUMMARY OF ESSENTIAL POINTS

◆ Use soundmakers within the hearing range of the child.

◆ Reduce background noise and visual distractions.

◆ Use appropriate language levels.

◆ Use familiar vocabulary.

◆ Look for consistent responses.

◆ Take into account the child's interests and preferences.

◆ Be aware of safety considerations.

◆ Record activities carefully.

HINTS FOR PARENTS

How to Help Your Child's Listening Skills

1 Only use sounds or soundmakers your child can hear. A speech and language therapist/clinician or teacher can help you choose the best sounds for your child.

2 Activities should be fun for you and your child. If it seems like hard work, stop! You may need to try again at a different time or change the activity.

3 Help your child to concentrate by keeping background noise quiet; for example, switch off the television or radio.

4 Remember that your child may not get it right the first time. As long as your child is not bored you can repeat activities as many times as you like.

5 You and your child will not be good playmates if you are hungry or sleepy. Choose a time that suits you as well as your child.

6 Make sure your child can see and hear you by sitting on the same level as your child.

7 Do not worry if your child seems to lose interest quickly. Listening can be tiring for some children. Several short play sessions are better than one long one.

DISCOVERING SOUND

SECTION 1

INTRODUCTION

THE ACTIVITIES in this section are designed to increase the child's awareness of sound in their everyday environment. There are many opportunities during the day for developing and reinforcing listening skills. Attending to sound is a natural part of some everyday activities. Everyday experience of sound is especially important for children with a hearing loss.

There is no specific teaching activity for this section. Instead guidelines are provided on ways to help the child to be aware of the sounds in their everyday environment.

Children enjoy listening to the noises and speech in their everyday environment and from an early age get pleasure from making their own sounds of gurgles, cries and babble. However some children may need help in attending to the many sounds that surround them. These activities will be particularly useful for children with a hearing loss or other communication difficulty. They will help the child to discover sound and soundmakers.

TEACHING
Guidelines

It is important that the child has an opportunity to hear and listen to a variety of sounds and noises throughout the day. Encourage the child to attend to sound by using the following prompts.

- ◆ *Seeing* – point to or show the soundmaker to the child. (Children who have difficulty turning need to be seated so that they are facing the right way.)

- ◆ *Touching* – let the child touch the soundmaker, holding a rattle, for example.

- ◆ *Feeling vibrations* – children who have difficulty hearing a sound will enjoy feeling vibrations associated with the sound, such as the vibrations of a wooden floor when a foot is tapped or the top of a washing machine on 'spin'.

 Avoid touching hot or moving parts of machinery.

- ◆ *Repetition* – make sure the child hears the sound as many times as possible in a variety of situations.

Remember: sounds should be audible to the child; soundmakers that are interesting to *look at* will quickly capture the child's attention.

ACTIVITIES FOR
School or Nursery

During the day vary the child's experience of sound by providing a variety of 'listening environments'. There should be opportunities to listen to sound, to make sound and to have times of quiet.

Activities for concentrated listening:

☐ story time

☐ tv show

☐ story time at the library

☐ music session

☐ singing songs

☐ saying nursery rhymes

☐ drama

☐ daily diary

☐ a taped story

Activities for quiet times:

☐ reading

☐ looking at picture books

☐ painting

☐ drawing

☐ sticking and gluing

☐ sewing

☐ knitting

☐ sleeping

☐ resting

Discover sound by listening:

- [ ] to a sea-shell
- [ ] through a stethoscope
- [ ] to music with headphones

- [ ] on a tin and string phone
- [ ] with hands cupped over ears
- [ ] to a music box

☐ Listen to everyday sounds

Draw the child's attention to everyday sounds and noises. Let the child see and touch the soundmaker and, if possible, make the sound herself. Sounds could include the doorbell, footsteps, water running in the sink, or a toilet flushing.

☐ Sound as a signal

Help the child to associate a sound with an activity: for example, a bell for meal time or the end of bike play.

ACTIVITIES FOR
Home

Help your child's awareness of everyday sounds by drawing her attention to the noises, sounds and voices around her. Children learn more about sound if they can see and touch the object making the sound.

☐ *Bath time*

At bath time show your child how to make a variety of sounds and noises:

- ◆ you can splash your hands in the water, or squeeze a wet sponge and let it dribble into the bath
- ◆ use bubble bath for your child to make lots of bubbles by swishing the water
- ◆ collect together toys that can be dropped with a plink-plonk into the water
- ◆ there are many cheap wind-up toys in various shapes and sizes that include boats, swimmers and frogs. Your child can wind them up and listen to the noises they make as they flap through the water

 Please note that water play should be supervised at all times.

☐ *Listening walk*

While walking to the shops, round to a friend's house or in the park talk to your child about the noises you hear on the way. Different routes will give your child a variety of listening experiences. You and your child can make some noises by banging a stick against a metal fence, splashing through puddles or kicking fallen leaves.

7

How many of these sounds has your child heard?

- ☐ footsteps on the pavement
- ☐ car engine
- ☐ washing flapping in the wind
- ☐ leaves rustling
- ☐ bird song
- ☐ your voice!
- ☐ echoing voices in the corridor
- ☐ key in the door
- ☐ washing up in the kitchen
- ☐ cutlery put away in the drawer
- ☐ running bath water
- ☐ dog barking
- ☐ ambulance siren
- ☐ toilet flushing
- ☐ doorbell
- ☐ door banging

Write down any other sounds your child has enjoyed.

☐ Everyday routines

Use sound to help your child anticipate activities; for example, before bath time you could splash the water with your hand. This will help your child to associate the sound with the activity.

Sounds &
SOUNDMAKERS

Section 14 lists a variety of sounds and noises. Those suggested under the following headings are particularly useful for discovery activities:

- ☐ musical instruments
- ☐ home sounds
- ☐ everyday objects
- ☐ human sounds
- ☐ environmental sounds
- ☐ action sounds

Discovering Sound
CHECKLIST

Child's name	

Date	Activity	Comments
Example **21.8.**	**Listening walk**	*Pointed at aircraft overhead after hearing noise.*

Early Listening Skills

P

EXPLORING SOUNDMAKERS

SECTION 2

INTRODUCTION

THIS SECTION has ideas for helping the child to make sounds with a variety of toys and soundmakers. The child is encouraged to be an active participant and to explore different ways of making sound. The games also involve anticipation and cause and effect.

There is no specific teaching activity for this section. Instead guidelines are provided on how to help the child use soundmakers.

This section will introduce the child to many new and exciting ways of making sounds. The activities encourage the child to explore soundmakers using sight and touch as well as hearing. Looking at, touching and holding a soundmaker will help the child to become more aware of the vibrations and source of the sound. She will learn to anticipate sound and start to make a connection between her own actions and the resulting noises.

TEACHING
Guidelines

The child can be encouraged to explore a variety of appropriate soundmakers, which should include everyday noise makers, musical instruments and the child's own voice. Concentrate on one soundmaker at a time.

Allow the child some space and time to initiate her own actions with the soundmaker. You can then follow her lead and help to expand her play. Show the child how one toy can be used to make sound in a variety of ways: for example, a tambourine can be banged, tapped or scratched (see 'Activities for School or Nursery'). Practise the same action on different instruments, so that in one session the child is blowing a whistle and in the next one she is blowing into a mouth organ (see 'Activities for Home').

Some children may need support from the adult to develop their exploration of soundmakers. Below are some ideas on ways to prompt a child who is having difficulty.

◆ *Modelling* – showing the child the appropriate actions. At first the child should try to copy the adult as she performs the action. Later, as the child's imitative skills develop, there can be a delay between the modelling and the child's attempts.

◆ *Repetition* – repeating for the child either the action or the sound.

◆ *Playing alongside* – carrying out the action with the child (who should be seated at your side).

◆ *Physical prompts* – helping the child physically carry out the action: for example, pressing her finger down on a button or holding her fingers around a shaker.

◆ *Gesture* – cueing the child by miming the appropriate action.

The games for school, nursery and home can be adapted for use as teaching activities.

ACTIVITIES FOR
School or Nursery

To make the most of your soundmakers:

◆ have a special time in the day for children to explore soundmakers and musical instruments;

◆ gather useful items together for a 'listening box' (see p248 for ideas);

◆ try to have pairs of instruments so you can play matching games;

◆ ask the children's families for ideas about musical instruments and soundmakers so that your collection represents various cultures and backgrounds.

Here are some ideas for helping children to explore the musical instruments and soundmakers.

☐ *Use one soundmaker in different ways*

Show the child the different ways sound can be made from one soundmaker: for example, a tambourine can be shaken, tapped, scratched or hit with a hard or soft blow.

☐ *Make different sounds by using different beaters*

Show the child how different sounds can be made when beaters are varied: for example, the difference between a drum struck by a rubber beater and a drum struck by a wooden beater. Try beaters made out of metal or ones covered with felt, and so on. Instead of drums use a glockenspiel or xylophone.

☐ *Make different sounds from different parts of an instrument*

Show the child the different sounds that can be made by using different parts of an instrument, such as the different sounds produced when the inner and then the outer edge of a drum are beaten. Other ideas include the inner and the outer edge of a tambourine, or different keys on a piano.

Explore the different pitch and volume of sounds

Let the child hear the difference between soundmakers that make quiet and loud sounds: for example, rice shaken in a yoghurt pot compared with two saucepan lids banging together. Compare the sounds of instruments with a low pitch, such as a drum, and a high pitch, such as cymbals.

Show the child how to make loud and quiet sounds with the same soundmaker: for example, a spoon gently stirred around a cup will be quieter than a spoon banged on the side of a cup.

Listening corner

Make a 'listening corner' where the children can listen to a number of different soundmakers. These could include stories and music on cassettes.

ACTIVITIES FOR
Home

Use toys and everyday objects from around the home to help your child explore a variety of sounds and soundmakers.

Make a sound by banging:

- ☐ two shells together
- ☐ a wooden spoon on a saucepan
- ☐ two wooden bricks together
- ☐ a wooden spoon on an upside-down tin
- ☐ plastic egg cups together
- ☐ a stick on a box
- ☐ your feet on the ground
- ☐ two saucepan lids together

Make a sound by tapping:

- ☐ a stick on a fir cone
- ☐ a bamboo stick on a porcelain bowl filled with water
- ☐ wooden sticks together
- ☐ your fingers on the table or on a tin tray
- ☐ pencils or pens together
- ☐ a stick on an empty plastic bottle
- ☐ a metal spoon on an upturned plastic flower pot

Make a sound by dropping:

- [ ] a ball into a bucket
- [ ] marbles into a tin
- [ ] toys into the bath
- [ ] cutlery into a tray
- [ ] buttons into a jar

Make a sound by shaking:

- [ ] a rattle
- [ ] your bunch of keys
- [ ] a tambourine
- [ ] a box of buttons (make sure the lid fits securely)
- [ ] a tin of rice or coffee
- [ ] toy bricks in an empty tin

Make a sound by kicking:

- [ ] toy balls with bells inside
- [ ] a musical frame
- [ ] an empty bucket
- [ ] your feet through leaves
- [ ] a ball against a wall
- [ ] a tower of toy bricks

Make a sound by scrunching:

- [ ] stiff paper
- [ ] greaseproof paper
- [ ] tracing paper
- [ ] cellophane from chocolate boxes

Make a sound by squeezing:

- ☐ squeaky toys
- ☐ a horn
- ☐ a hooter

Make a sound by blowing:

- ☐ into an empty bottle
- ☐ on tissue paper over a comb
- ☐ a toy trumpet
- ☐ a whistle
- ☐ a raspberry!
- ☐ a mouth organ
- ☐ a paper horn
- ☐ on wind chimes
- ☐ on a musical mobile
- ☐ a kiss

Make a sound by using your voice to:

- ☐ hum
- ☐ laugh
- ☐ talk
- ☐ sing

Encourage your child to copy you. If your child makes a sound or noise, copy her! You can make it into a game by adding a new sound: for example, "bbb" – "bbb boo".

Sounds &
SOUNDMAKERS

Section 14 lists a variety of soundmakers. Those suggested under the following headings are particularly useful for exploration activities:

- [ ] musical instruments
- [ ] home sounds
- [ ] everyday objects
- [ ] environmental sounds
- [ ] action sounds

Exploring Soundmakers
CHECKLIST

Child's name

Date	Soundmaker	Sound made by:	Comments
Example 20.7.	Drum	Tapping with fingers	Copied tapping when alongside adult.

21

SOUND OR SILENCE?

SECTION 3

INTRODUCTION

CHILDREN WITH a hearing loss may have difficulty in detecting sound and distinguishing the start and finish of a sound. This section is specifically aimed at developing skills of auditory detection in these children. However, other children with listening difficulties will also benefit from the games which are useful for improving concentration and memory.

The activities include a range of stimuli, from noises made by everyday objects to representational sounds and speech. This provides an opportunity for the child to experience a variety of sounds produced within appropriate contexts.

It is not necessary for the child to understand what the sound is, or even to know whether it is the same as or different from other sounds. Use a variety of sounds, but present only one at a time and avoid making the child have to choose, otherwise the activity will become an auditory recognition task.

The activities aim to develop the child's awareness of sound, drawing attention to the start and finish of sounds and developing the child's ability to tell the difference between sound and silence.

Musical Instruments
TEACHING ACTIVITY
'Beat that Drum'

You will need:

*a drum with a loud
and deep sound;
a beater;
a small screen;
hoops on a stick.*

Useful words
and phrases:

*look; listen; drum;
noise; no noise;
hoop; stick; beat.*

1 Introduce the drum by showing it to the child and making some sounds. Let the child have a turn at playing it.

2 Play a beat on the drum and place a hoop on the stick. (The sound and the placing of the hoop should coincide so that the child associates the action with the drum beat.)

3 Let the child have the next turn. Play another beat but this time help the child to place the hoop on the stick.

4 Repeat this several times with the child watching and listening until she is consistently placing a hoop on the stick.

5 Hide the drum behind the screen.

6 Give the child a hoop to hold ready and tell her to listen very hard for the noise of the drum. When she hears it she must put the hoop on the stick.

7 Avoid giving any unintentional clues when you make the drum beat, such as raised eyebrows, arm movements.

8 If the child has difficulty with the task, make several drum beats and increase the volume.

9 If she continues to have difficulty, let her watch again, until she is ready for an auditory task only.

To increase the complexity of the activity:
◆ use fewer repetitions of the drum beat;
◆ make the sound of the drum quieter;
◆ increase the distance between you and the child.

Variations
◆ Let the child take a turn at making the sound for you to place the hoop on the stick.
◆ Ask the child to perform different actions when she hears the drum beat, for example to clap her hands or raise her arms in the air.
◆ Ask the child to move in different ways when she hears the drum beat, for example to hop, take a large stride or stand up.
◆ Try using other simple construction toys instead of hoops on a stick.

Musical Instruments
ACTIVITIES FOR
School or Nursery

At first let the children see you turn the music on and off or play a note on an instrument. Later you can hide the soundmaker so the children are relying on their listening skills alone. These games will help the children to respond to sounds made by musical instruments. Choose one musical instrument or soundmaker for each game.

☐ *Action and movement games*

Using one musical instrument or musical soundmaker, ask the children to perform an action or movement when the instrument is played. Actions could include clapping their hands or raising their arms in the air. Movements could include standing up or sitting down, taking a large stride, a hop or a skip.

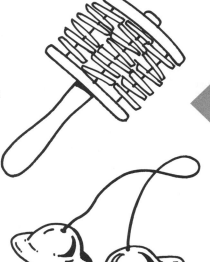

☐ *Musical statues*

The children move around to the sound of a musical instrument or soundmaker and freeze into a statue when it stops. Make the periods of silence between sounds longer and longer so it becomes more and more difficult for the children to stay still.

☐ *Musical bumps*

This is a variation of musical statues but in this game children sit down as soon as the music stops.

☐ *Musical chairs*

A group of children can play musical chairs. They must move around to the music and then sit on a chair when the music stops. The catch is that a chair is taken away each time and one child is 'out' when she loses her seat.

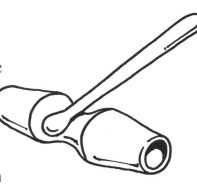

☐ *Vice versa*

Try playing musical chairs and statues with the child moving around when there is no sound, and stopping when the music is playing.

☐ *Sound or silence in everyday routines*

Use the start or the end of a sound to signal an activity; for example, the children have to wait until you finish ringing a bell before they line up for outside play.

Help your child by letting her watch as you turn the music on or off or when you make a sound. Later she can play the games by listening alone. These games will help your child to learn the difference between sound and no sound. Choose one musical instrument or soundmaker for each game.

☐ *Musical chairs*

Your child and some family members or a group of children at a party can play musical chairs. They must move around to the sound of the music and then sit on a chair when the music stops. The catch is that a chair is taken away each time and one person is out when she loses her seat.

☐ *Music box*

You will need a wind-up music box or a radio. Encourage your child to make her doll or teddy dance to the music. When the music stops the doll or teddy falls to the floor.

☐ *Jack in the box*

Let your child play the Jack in Jack in the box. You will need a large cardboard box. Your child hides in the box and waits for the signal. Make a loud sound by banging a wooden spoon on an upturned biscuit tin. Encourage your child to pop out when she hears the sound. The top of the box can have a loose-fitting lid, attached on one side, to make it more fun for her to 'pop' out.

☐ *Music on the radio or television*

Draw your child's attention to the start and the finish of musical sounds, such as a song ending on the radio or the end of the theme music of her favourite television programme.

Sounds & SOUNDMAKERS

Try using a variety of musical instruments or music makers. (Choose instruments or soundmakers where there is a clear difference between sound and no sound.) Some examples:

☐ hand bell

☐ music on a record player

☐ music box

☐ music on a radio

☐ music on a cassette player

☐ music on television

☐ musical toy

☐ drum

☐ wooden agogo

☐ tulip block

☐ sonar resonator tone bars

Home-made musical instruments:

☐ empty biscuit tin and wooden spoon (drum)

☐ two saucepan lids banged together

☐ two sticks to tap together

☐ a cardboard trumpet to blow through

Talk to your child's speech and language therapist/clinician or teacher about the musical instruments or musical soundmakers that interest you and your child. Ask them to tick appropriate instruments from the above list.

Everyday Sounds from Home
TEACHING ACTIVITY
'Wakey Wakey'

You will need:

a puppet with a large mouth that opens and closes; a blanket.

Useful words and phrases:

listen; look; "Wakey wakey"; puppet; naughty; blanket; sleeping.

1 Tell the child that you are going to play a game with a puppet. Explain that the puppet is very naughty and he keeps trying to wake up people when they are sleeping.

2 Ask the child to pretend to be asleep by lying down under the blanket. (At first it is important that she keeps her eyes open so she can watch the puppet.)

3 Tell her to listen and watch carefully. When the puppet calls, "Wakey wakey" she must jump up quickly.

4 When you have the child's attention, call, "Wakey wakey" and manipulate the puppet's mouth. Encourage her to jump up if she does not respond immediately.

5 When the child is confident with the activity, use voice only. Make sure the child's eyes are closed or position yourself out of sight.

6 Call out, "Wakey wakey".

7 If the child fails to respond even after repetitions, encourage the child to watch and listen as you call "Wakey wakey" again.

8 Continue with the game until the child is responding consistently without looking.

To increase the complexity of the activity:
◆ use fewer repetitions of "Wakey wakey";
◆ make your voice quieter;
◆ increase the distance between you and the child.

Variations
◆ Give the child an action to carry out when she hears "Wakey wakey"; for example, yawning or stretching arms.
◆ Let the child have a turn at holding the naughty puppet and calling out, "Wakey wakey".
◆ If you are playing this with a group, the other children can be encouraged to join in as a chorus and tell the naughty puppet off when he wakes the child up.

Everyday Sounds from Home
ACTIVITIES FOR
School or Nursery

At first let the children see you make the sound. Later you can make the sound out of sight so the children are relying on their listening skills. Remember to use only one sound at a time, otherwise the child will need to know the sound in order to produce the appropriate action.

☐ Home corner

Join the children in the home corner and play some sound games. The child could open a door when a knocker sounds or pick up the phone when a bell rings.

☐ Puppets

Use a puppet that the child has to wake up when you call, "Wakey wakey". Other ways of waking the puppet up could be a book dropping or an alarm clock ringing.

☐ Knock knock – it's the postman!

One child brings the other children surprise presents. They must wait for the knock on the door before opening it for the postman. (The presents can be as simple as a picture cut from a magazine or a small sweet.)

Everyday Sounds from Home
ACTIVITIES FOR
Home

Help your child by letting her see the soundmaker or watch your face as you make the sound. These games will help your child to respond to everyday sounds. Choose one sound for each game.

☐ ***Answer that, please!***

Encourage your child to be aware of noises in the home, such as the doorbell or knocker, or the telephone ringing. Help her to pick up the phone or open the door. It does not matter if your child confuses the sounds at this stage. The aim is for her to show that she has heard a sound.

☐ ***Knock knock***

Play this game with your child. Your child must open the door to you when she hears you knock. (Use the lounge, kitchen or bedroom door.) Give her a surprise present each time, such as a balloon, a paper hat or a sweet, or blow some bubbles. She only gets a present if she waits for you to knock. Try to make the time she has to wait longer and longer.

☐ ***Toy telephone***

Record the sound of the phone ringing on a cassette player. You can play a 'pretend' game with your child, using the tape. When your child hears the phone on the tape she must pick up a toy telephone.

☐ ***Doll play***

Play 'pretend' play. Put dolly to sleep. Show your child how to wake her up by calling her name or saying, "Wakey wakey". Can your child wake dolly when you say the name? Try this game using an alarm clock or radio to wake dolly.

Sounds &
SOUNDMAKERS

Try using a variety of sounds. (Choose sounds or soundmakers where there is a clear difference between sound and no sound.) A list of everyday sounds might include the following:

- ☐ the ring of the alarm clock
- ☐ music or chat on the radio
- ☐ music from a cassette player
- ☐ a music box
- ☐ objects being dropped, such as a book banging on a table, or a door slamming
- ☐ the door knocker

It may be easier to record some sounds, such as:

- ☐ the ring of the telephone or the doorbell
- ☐ the sound of the television
- ☐ someone playing the piano
- ☐ hammering
- ☐ drilling
- ☐ doors banging

Talk to your child's speech and language therapist/clinician or teacher about the sounds or soundmakers that interest you and your child. Ask them to tick appropriate sounds or soundmakers from the above list.

P

Human Sounds
TEACHING ACTIVITY
'Dolly has a Cold'

You will need:

a doll; some tissues; a screen (a screen can be made by placing opaque material in an embroidery frame).

Useful words and phrases:

look; listen; sneeze; wipe; cold; tissue; dolly; nose.

1 Show the doll to the child. Explain that poor dolly has a nasty cold and she needs some help with blowing her nose.

2 Ask her to watch and listen.

3 Make an exaggerated sneeze. Give the child some tissues and ask her to wipe dolly's nose.

4 When the child has the idea of the game, try with listening only.

5 Hide your face with the embroidery frame and ask the child to listen carefully. Tell her she must wipe dolly's nose as soon as she hears a sneeze.

6 Make a sneezing noise but be careful not to give any clues by moving your head.

7 If she has difficulty with the task, repeat the sound of the sneezing.

8 If she still does not respond correctly, let her see as you sneeze and draw her attention to the noise.

9 Repeat the activity several times.

To increase the complexity of the activity:
◆ use fewer repetitions of the sneezes;
◆ make your sneeze quieter;
◆ increase the distance between you and the child.

Variations
◆ Ask the child to respond in different ways, such as saying "Bless you", or giving dolly some medicine.
◆ Record the sneezes on a tape recorder.
◆ A group of children can take turns at sneezing.
◆ Use other human sounds or simple words with appropriate actions.

Human Sounds

ACTIVITIES FOR
School or Nursery

At first let the children watch your face as you make the sound or say the word. Later you can hide your face behind a large piece of card, so the children are relying on their listening skills alone. At this stage the children are not expected to know the sounds or words. The aim is to teach the children to respond to a sound or voice.

☐ *'Ring-a-Ring-of-Roses'*

Sing 'Ring-a-Ring-of-Roses' but make the children wait for the sneeze before they make the appropriate action.

☐ *Races*

Play race games. The children must wait for the word 'go' as a signal to start the race.

☐ *Up game*

The children crouch down on the floor. When you shout out "Up" they all jump up together. Anybody who is too quick or too slow is 'out'.

☐ *'Pretend' play*

Using a doll or teddy ask the children to carry out actions with the doll when they hear a sound. Choose one sound and one action to work on at a time. Examples of suitable sounds and actions are blowing dolly's nose after she sneezes or patting her back when she coughs.

ACTIVITIES FOR
Home

Help your child by letting her see your face as you make a sound or say a word. These games will help your child to tell the difference between sound and silence. Choose one sound or word for each game. At this stage your child is not expected to know the sounds or words. The aim is to teach her to respond to a sound or voice.

☐ *Poor dolly*

Show the child how to give dolly or teddy a cuddle when you say "Ah". Encourage her to wait until you have made the sound before she picks up dolly or teddy for a cuddle.

☐ *Wave 'bye-bye'*

Help your child wave 'bye-bye' to friends and family. Always use the words as you wave. Can she wave when just the words, without a gesture, are used?

☐ *'Ring-a-Ring-of-Roses'*

Sing this song and encourage your child to make the sound of sneezing and to blow her nose. Sing the song for her and see if she can do the actions in the right place.

☐ *Build a tower*

Help your child to build a tower. Say, "Ready, steady..." and then help her knock down the tower when you say" Go!' in a loud voice. Next time, see if she can wait for the word 'go' without your help.

☐ *Peek-a-boo*

Hide your face behind your hands. Shout out "Boo!" as you uncover your face. Encourage your child to copy you. Help her keep her face covered until you shout "Boo!".

P

Sounds &
SOUNDMAKERS

Try to use a variety of human sounds. Suggestions for sounds and accompanying actions are:

- ☐ "bye-bye" – wave bye-bye
- ☐ crying – pat dolly's head or give dolly a cuddle
- ☐ "shhh" – dolly is talking when she should be going to sleep
- ☐ "I'm hungry" – give dolly a 'pretend' biscuit
- ☐ moan in pain – rub dolly's tummy
- ☐ cough – cover dolly's mouth
- ☐ "boo" – uncover face
- ☐ "go" – knock down bricks or start a race
- ☐ "up" and "down" – carry out appropriate action
- ☐ sneeze – wipe dolly's nose or hold own nose

Talk to your child's speech and language therapist/clinician or teacher about the sounds or soundmakers that interest you and your child. Ask them to tick appropriate sounds or soundmakers from the above list.

Everyday Objects
TEACHING ACTIVITY
'Shake the Noise'

You will need:

a wooden brick;
two identical tins with
removable lids.

**Useful words
and phrases:**

look; listen; tin; brick;
shake; noise; silent; lid;
empty; full.

1 Show the child the two identical tins. Shake each one and then remove the lids to show that they are empty.

2 Let the child see as you put the brick in one of the empty tins. Replace the lid and shake it so the child hears the noise it makes.

3 Encourage the child to shake the tin and make a noise.

4 Move the two tins around so that the child is not sure which one has the brick.

5 Shake one tin for several seconds and then shake the other tin for several seconds.

6 Ask the child which tin has the brick. (Avoid letting her shake the tin herself as she may be able to guess from the weight of the tin.)

7 If the child seems unsure, shake the tin for a longer time. If she continues to have difficulty, shake the empty tin and open the lid, then shake the full one and open the lid.

8 Repeat steps 4–6.

9 Let the child open the tin when she has made the correct choice.

To increase the complexity of the activity:

◆ shake the tin for a shorter period of time;
◆ use objects that make a quieter sound;
◆ increase the distance between you and the child.

Variations

◆ Vary pitch and volume by using different objects in the containers; for example, rice will have a different sound from marbles.
◆ Vary pitch and volume by using different containers; for example, marbles in a tin will have a different sound from marbles in a plastic container.
◆ Put pictures on the front of the tins. The child has to name or sign the picture to indicate which container has the brick.
◆ Pretend to be a magician. Try wearing a top hat and waving a magic wand!

Everyday Objects

ACTIVITIES FOR
School or Nursery

You will need several shakers. You can make your own or use a commercial product. These games are for sorting those shakers that make a noise from those that are silent. The sounds do not have to be matched or the materials which make the sound identified.

☐ *Sorting games*

Use several shakers. Ask the children to sort them into groups of noisy shakers and silent shakers.

☐ *Find the noisy shaker*

Ask one child to leave the room while you give a noisy shaker to one child and a silent shaker to another. On the child's return to the room she listens to each shaker in turn. Can she guess who has the noisy shaker?

SECTION 3

Everyday Objects
ACTIVITIES FOR
Home

Help your child by letting her see the soundmaker. These games will help your child to learn the difference between sound and silence. Choose one everyday object for each game.

Find the brick

To play this game you will need two identical cardboard boxes with lids and one large wooden brick. Show your child the empty boxes. Shake each one and then remove the lids to show that they are empty. Let your child see as you put the brick in one of the empty boxes. Replace the lid and shake it so she hears the noise it makes. Encourage her to shake the box and make a noise.

Next move the two boxes around so that the child is not sure which one has the brick. Can your child find the brick by listening to the boxes? Try this game using different containers and other toys or objects.

Full or empty

Ask your child to help you sort your shopping. Choose foods that make a noise when the packet is shaken, such as cereals, tea, or coffee in a jar. Can your child tell the difference between an empty packet and a full one? Let her shake the packet if she has difficulty with hearing the noise.

Sounds &
SOUNDMAKERS

The following items can be placed in shakers:

- ☐ coins
- ☐ toy plastic animals
- ☐ small toys
- ☐ model vehicles
- ☐ safety pins or paper clips
- ☐ keys
- ☐ beads

- ☐ matches (spent)
- ☐ paper strips
- ☐ pegs
- ☐ curtain hooks
- ☐ pebbles or stones
- ☐ cotton reels

! **Always be extremely careful with small objects which may be swallowed accidentally by young children. Items should be placed in shakers with *secure* lids. If in any doubt, use larger objects or toys. Specialist children's stores, such as Mothercare, sell a device for checking whether objects are small enough to be swallowed.**

Talk to your child's speech and language therapist/clinician or teacher about the everyday objects that interest you and your child. Ask them to tick appropriate objects from the above list.

Representational Sounds
TEACHING ACTIVITY
'Farmyard'

You will need:

a farmyard model;
several plastic shapes
of cows; a box.

**Useful words
and phrases:**

look; listen; cow;
'moo'; farm;
sound or noise.

1 Set up the farmyard model on a table. Show the child the toy cows and allow her to play with them for a few minutes.

2 Explain that you are going to play a listening game. Place the cows in a box and put this to one side.

3 Give the child one of the toy cows and tell her to listen carefully. Make a mooing sound and prompt her to place the toy cow in the farmyard.

4 Repeat the game with another toy cow. This time, see if the child can place the cow in the farmyard without any prompts.

5 Next cover your mouth with your hand when you make the sound, so that the child has to rely on listening alone.

6 If the child has difficulty, repeat the sound and then prompt her to place the cow in the farmyard.

7 Continue the game until all the cows are placed in the farmyard.

To increase the complexity of the activity:
◆ use fewer repetitions of the animal sounds;
◆ use animal sounds that are shorter;
◆ use animal sounds that are quieter.

Variations
◆ Introduce other animal sounds, but remember to only use one animal sound at a time.

◆ Play this game with a group of children. The sounds will be repeated many times, increasing the listening practice for the child. An older child can be included in the group to model the appropriate responses for the other children.

◆ Record the sounds on a tape recorder.

◆ Make a paper pathway for the model farm that leads from the field to the barn. The child has to move the animal along the pathway one square at a time when she hears the noise.

Representational Sounds
ACTIVITIES FOR
School or Nursery

At first let the children watch your face as you make the sounds. Later you can hide your face behind a large piece of card so the children are relying on their listening skills alone. These activities will help the child to learn the difference between sound and silence. Remember to use only one sound at a time, otherwise the child will need to know the sound in order to produce the appropriate action.

☐ Posting box

Gather together several pictures of the same animal. Each child must wait for you to make the sound of the animal first, before posting a picture in the box.

☐ Animals on the farm

Set out a model farm or a farm layout. Choose one animal and a suitable sound. These could include a 'moo' for a cow, a 'neigh' for a horse and so on. Show the children how to place one of the animals in the farm when you say a sound. Let each child have a turn.

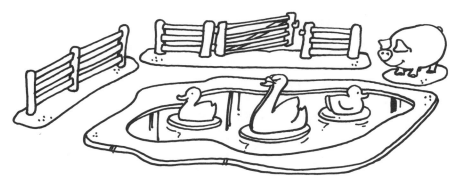

☐ Small doll play

Use the *Playmobile Park* or similar miniature doll material to play this game. Choose one sound and action to play with the child. This could be the sound 'wheel!', with dolly having a slide, a swing or a spin on the roundabout. Make the sound and encourage the child to carry out the action.

☐ Home corner

Play listening games with the children in the home corner. Choose one sound and an appropriate action, such as 'ding ding' for the phone. Make the sound and encourage the child to pick up the phone and say, "Hello".

SECTION 3

Representational Sounds
ACTIVITIES FOR
Home

Help your child by letting her see your face as you make a sound. (Later you can hide your face.) These games will help your child to learn the difference between sound and silence. Choose one sound for your child to listen for in each game.

☐ *Park the car*

You will need a toy car and a garage. (An old shoe box can be turned upside down and a hole put in one side to make a 'pretend' garage.) Give your child the car and make a sound like a car engine – "vroom!". Help your child to push the car into the garage. Next time, see if she can wait for the sound before she pushes the car.

☐ *Jumping frogs*

Collect together some toy frogs or make some out of cardboard. Make one of the frogs jump in a bucket when you make a croaking sound. Encourage your child to wait for the sound before she helps the frog jump. (Add water and some leaves to make it like a real pond!)

☐ *Animal sounds*

Play a game with animal puppets or soft toys. A cat can be stroked when you say "Miaow". A dog can jump up and down when you say "Woof-woof".

☐ *In the dog house*

Use a soft toy and an old box for a kennel. Give your child the toy dog and say "Woof-woof". Help your child to put the dog in its kennel. Next time, see if she can wait for the sound before she puts the dog in the kennel.

☐ *Ring-a-ding*

Use a toy telephone or the real thing. Make a ringing sound. Encourage your child to pick up the phone and say, "Hello". Make the phone ring for dolly, teddy, daddy, mummy and anyone else who wants a call.

☐ *On the slide*

Take your child on the slide at the park. She must wait for you to call out "Whee!", before she slides down. At home she can play the same game with her dolls or teddies. Use a shiny book or piece of wood for the slide.

Sounds &
SOUNDMAKERS

Here are some suggestions for sounds and toys that can be used to represent feelings, objects or situations:

- ☐ "whee!" – push dolly down the slide
- ☐ "whee!" – dolly has a spin on a roundabout
- ☐ "beep beep" – drive a car along a road
- ☐ "ding ding" – ring the bell on the bus
- ☐ "vroom" – drive a bus or car into a garage
- ☐ "choo choo" – push the train through the tunnel
- ☐ "chchch choo" – train rushing along the track
- ☐ "tick tock" – turn the clock on its face
- ☐ "ding ding" – answer the telephone
- ☐ "tweet tweet" – pop a toy bird in a cage
- ☐ animal sounds

Talk to your child's speech and language therapist/clinician or teacher about the sounds and toys that interest you and your child. Ask them to tick appropriate sounds and toys from the above list.

Sound or Silence
CHECKLIST

Child's name	

Date	Activity	Sound	Comments
Example **21.9.**	**Music bumps**	**Radio**	**Needs to watch for sound being switched on or off.**

SIMPLE DISCRIMINATION

SECTION 4

INTRODUCTION

THESE ACTIVITIES are designed to develop the child's ability to make simple discriminations between sounds. The activities require the child to decide whether two sounds are the same or different. This is the first step towards the ability to discriminate one sound from another. The activities are suitable for children who have not yet developed sound recognition. They are also useful for improving concentration and memory.

At this stage the child does not have to show any recognition of the sound, so, for example, she might be aware that two beats on a drum are the same sound without being able to identify that a musical instrument made the sound.

Musical Instruments
TEACHING ACTIVITY
'Spot the Difference'

You will need:

two identical shakers;
one drum;
a screen.

Useful words and phrases:

look; listen; same;
different; shaker(s);
drum; first; last;
second; sound.

1 Introduce the shakers to the child. Talk about how they look and sound the same. Let the child have a turn at playing with them and comparing the sounds.

2 Put the shakers to one side when the child has finished playing and introduce the drum. Let the child have a turn at banging it.

3 Next choose one shaker and make a sound, then beat the drum. Point out to the child how the sound is different.

4 Explain to the child that you are going to play a listening game. Place one of the shakers in front of the child but out of reach. Place the other shaker and drum behind the screen.

5 Make sure the child is ready and then tell her to listen carefully. Make a sound with the shaker in sight and then a second sound behind the screen using either the other shaker or the drum. (Some children may need to hear the shaker two or three times *before* a sound is made by the instrument behind the screen.)

6 Ask the child if the sounds are the same or different.

7 Let the child see the second soundmaker when she has chosen. If she has made a mistake, play the sounds again.

8 Repeat until the child has had several turns.

To increase the complexity of the activity:
◆ introduce instruments that sound increasingly similar;
◆ introduce a delay before making the second sound.

Variations
◆ Vary the musical instruments.
◆ Record two or three sounds from musical instruments on tape. Ask the child to put up her hand when the sound is different. Always keep the first sound the same; that is, A A, A B, A B B or A A B B.

Musical Instruments
ACTIVITIES FOR
School or Nursery

These games will help the child to learn how sounds can be the same or different. The children do not need to identify the musical instruments. Let the children see you making the sounds before playing the games with the instruments hidden.

☐ *Find the matching instrument*

(You will need pairs of matching instruments to play this game.) Hide one set of instruments behind a screen and place the matching instruments on a table. The child chooses an instrument from the table. She must listen while you play an instrument behind the screen. If the sounds are the same she can put the instrument away in a box. If not, another child has a turn.

☐ *Team games*

Divide the children into two teams and provide them with pairs of matching maracas divided equally between the two groups. Can each child pair up with the other child who has the same sound? When the children have found a partner they sit together on the floor.

Try giving the children a time limit. The losers are the children who do not find their matching partner in time.

☐ *Children as musicians*

Ask two children from the group to go behind a screen and each choose a musical instrument from a box of assorted matching pairs. Each child takes it in turn to play her instrument behind the screen. The other children have to decide whether the sounds are the same or different.

Section 4: Simple Discrimination

ACTIVITIES FOR
Home

These games will help your child to learn about the way sounds can be the same or different. Let your child watch as you make the sounds. Later you can try the games with the instruments hidden.

Collect together some home-made instruments:

- ☐ A drum can be made from an empty biscuit tin, with a wooden spoon for the beater

- ☐ A gong can be made by hanging up a saucepan lid or an old frying pan

- ☐ Two wooden sticks can be tapped together

- ☐ Thread some silver milk bottle tops on a string to make a shaker

Try to have two of each instrument – one for you and one for your child. Make a sound. Encourage your child to copy you. Draw her attention to the fact that the sounds are the same. Play different instruments to show her the sounds are different.

Sounds & SOUNDMAKERS

Try using a variety of musical instruments or music makers such as the following in simple discrimination games:

- [ ] cymbals
- [ ] maracas
- [ ] drum
- [ ] shaker
- [ ] wood blocks and mallet
- [ ] tone bars

- [ ] jingle bells
- [ ] triangles
- [ ] castanets
- [ ] tambourines
- [ ] pali blocks and mallet

Home-made musical instruments:

- [ ] empty biscuit tin and a wooden spoon (drum)
- [ ] frying pan or saucepan lid (gong)
- [ ] rattle
- [ ] silver foil bottle tops threaded on string
- [ ] two sticks to tap together
- [ ] flower pot and stick to tap together

Talk to your child's speech and language therapist/clinician or teacher about the musical instruments that interest you and your child. Ask them to tick appropriate instruments from the above list.

Everyday Objects
TEACHING ACTIVITY
'Sound Pairs'

You will need:

several pairs of identical shakers filled with different everyday objects.

Useful words and phrases:

shaker; same; different; listen; pair; two.

1 Choose one matching pair of shakers.

2 Demonstrate to the child that they sound the same.

3 Next bring out a different shaker that does not match. Put this with one of the original shakers and demonstrate to the child that the sounds made by the two shakers are different.

4 Pick out another two shakers.

5 Shake the containers for the child, otherwise she might guess they are the same or different by their weight.

6 Can she tell you if the sound is the same or different?

7 If she has difficulty, help her by letting her listen to a third shaker that is different (D) or the same (S), depending on what combination she has picked; that is, use a different shaker if the pair are matching (S S <u>D</u>) and the matching shaker to one of a non-matching pair (<u>S</u> D <u>S</u>).

To increase the complexity of the activity:

◆ gradually increase the number of shakers (maximum ten pairs);
◆ introduce objects that sound increasingly similar;
◆ introduce a delay before the second sound is made.

Variations

◆ Put identifying marks on the bottom of the containers so that the child is able to check if she is correct.

◆ Play sound Pelmanism. Place several shakers on the table. Take it in turns with the child to select two shakers. The winner is the one with the most matching pairs.

Everyday Objects
ACTIVITIES FOR
School or Nursery

These games will help the child practise her skills in discriminating whether sounds are the same or different. The children do not need to identify the everyday objects.

☐ *Group games*

You will need several shakers which have matching sounds. Each child takes it in turn to pick two shakers. Either an adult or another child must shake the containers, otherwise the weight of the containers might give a clue. The child keeps any shakers that have a matching sound. The winner is the child with the most containers.

☐ *Team games*

Divide the children into two teams to play the above game. A child from each team has a turn at selecting a pair of shakers and deciding if they sound the same. They keep those that do match. The winning team is the one with the most shakers.

☐ *Find the odd one out*

You will need several matching shakers. Divide the children into two teams. Choose two matching shakers. Place one with two other, non-matching, shakers. (Do this out of sight from the children.) Give the other matching shaker to one of the team members. Can she find its matching shaker amongst the three? Each team takes it in turn. (Keep alternating the shakers.) The winning team is the one with the most matching pairs.

☐ *Pairs*

Ask one child to choose a shaker from several matching pairs. While she leaves the room, give one shaker each to two children in the group. (One of the shakers will match the one chosen by the child who has left the room.) On her return she must listen to both shakers and decide which one is the same as her own.

SECTION 4

ACTIVITIES FOR
Home

These games will help your child to learn about the way sounds can be the same or different.

☐ *Sounds the same*

Draw your child's attention to the way two objects make the same sound. Make one sound, followed by a matching sound. Try some of the following:
◆ dropping two coins
◆ shaking two boxes of paper clips
◆ shaking two bunches of keys
◆ shaking pegs in tins

☐ *Copy a sound*

If your child makes a sound with an object, try to make the same sound: if your child drops a book, show her how you can make the same sound by dropping another book.

Sounds &
SOUNDMAKERS

You may carry out simple discrimination games with a variety of everyday objects such as the following:

- [ ] keys
- [ ] coins
- [ ] spoon in a cup or glass
- [ ] book shutting or dropping
- [ ] scrunchy paper
- [ ] scissors cutting paper
- [ ] pencil being sharpened
- [ ] water being poured
- [ ] knife scraping on a plate
- [ ] watch with an electronic bleep
- [ ] pencil scribbling
- [ ] fingers tapping on a table or window
- [ ] door banging

Section 4: Simple Discrimination

There are numerous everyday objects and small toys that can be used in shakers. These include:

- [ ] toy plastic animals
- [ ] small toys
- [ ] model vehicles
- [ ] safety pins
- [ ] paper clips
- [ ] keys
- [ ] coins
- [ ] beads
- [ ] matches (spent)
- [ ] paper strips

- [ ] pegs
- [ ] curtain hooks
- [ ] expanded polystyrene
- [ ] pebbles
- [ ] stones
- [ ] cotton reels
- [ ] sand
- [ ] clay
- [ ] *Plasticine*

! **Always be extremely careful with small objects which may be swallowed accidentally by young children. Items should be placed in shakers with *secure* lids. If in any doubt, use larger objects or toys. Specialist children's stores, such as Mothercare, sell a device for checking whether objects are small enough to be swallowed.**

Talk to your child's speech therapist/clinician or teacher about the everyday objects that interest you and your child. Ask them to tick appropriate objects from the above list.

Simple Discrimination
CHECKLIST

Child's name

Date	Activity	Comments
Example 30.9.	*Musical instruments*	*Copied banging on a drum.*

SOUND RECOGNITION

SECTION 5

INTRODUCTION

THE ACTIVITIES in this section are designed to develop the child's ability to recognize sound and give meaning to it. Children should be able to detect sound and make simple discriminations before attempting these games. At this stage the child is able to identify sounds without necessarily having the ability to name the sound or the source of the sound.

The activities require a range of responses, including matching of soundmakers, responding to a sound signal and identifying taped sounds. They include activities that are suitable for children with limited speech who can identify soundmakers by selecting objects or pictures. These games are also useful for improving concentration and memory.

Children will begin to attach meaning to sound by associating what they hear with the source of the sound. The ability to identify sound is essential to the development of the child's listening and language skills, which children with communication difficulties often need to improve.

Children who are able to identify sounds without having the ability to name the sound or soundmaker may use sound rather than words to represent objects and events, such as 'quack quack' for duck, and 'whee!' for going down a slide.

Musical Instruments
TEACHING ACTIVITY
'Action to Sound'

You will need:

a drum; bells;
a large floor space.

**Useful words
and phrases:**

look; listen;
clap (hands);
stamp feet;
wait; drum;
bells.

1 This activity is best carried out in a large room where the child will have open space to move around.

2 Demonstrate the sound that the drum makes. Let the child have a turn at playing it.

3 Explain that you want her to stamp her feet when she hears the drum beat. Play the drum and encourage her to stamp her feet.

4 When she is confident with this task, introduce the bells and demonstrate the sound that they make.

5 Let the child have a turn at playing them. (For some children with poor attention skills it would be better to put the first instrument away before showing the other one.)

6 Explain to the child that you want her to clap her hands when she hears the bells. Shake the bells and encourage her to clap her hands.

7 When she is confident with this task, repeat the activity, using both instruments. Make a sound with the drum. Does she remember to stamp her feet? Make a sound with the bells. Does she remember to clap her hands?

8 When the child is responding appropriately with the instruments in sight, hide the drum and bells behind a screen.

9 Ask her to listen carefully.

10 Choose an instrument and make a sound. If she makes a mistake, repeat the sound. If she continues to have difficulty, show her the instrument and encourage her to make the appropriate action. Now try with the instrument hidden again.

11 Continue with the activity until the child is confidently matching action to sound.

To increase the complexity of the activity:

◆ increase the number of musical instruments (seven to eight maximum);

◆ introduce musical instruments that sound increasingly similar;

◆ ask the child to respond to a sequence of musical instruments (three maximum);

◆ use less familiar sounds;

◆ introduce a delay before the child is allowed to respond.

Variations

◆ Introduce different actions for the child, such as waving her hands, rubbing her tummy, lifting her arms up or touching the floor.

◆ Let the child have a turn at making the sounds. You carry out the appropriate action.

Musical Instruments
ACTIVITIES FOR
School or Nursery

These activities will help the child to respond to different musical instruments. At first let the children watch as you make the sound with the instrument. Later you can hide the instrument so the children are relying on their listening skills alone.

☐ *Matching the instrument to a picture*

Place a picture of a musical instrument on each nursery table. Use real instruments that match the pictures to make the sounds. The children must listen for the sound of their instrument before they can sit down at the table.

☐ *Action and movement games*

Teach the children to perform an action or movement to the sound of a musical instrument or musical soundmaker. Start with one instrument and one action or movement. Actions could include clapping hands, standing up or waving arms in the air. Movements could include walking very fast, hopping, taking large strides, skipping or dancing. Once the children are confident with one instrument you can introduce another. The children are 'out' if they perform the wrong action to the sound.

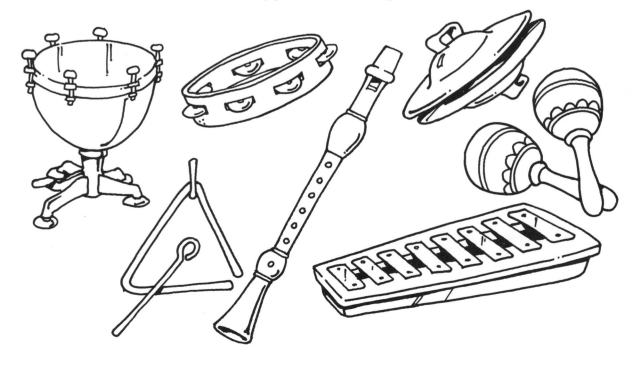

P

Team games

Divide the children into two teams. Each team must listen for a sound from a musical instrument. For example, team A listens for a drum and team B listens for a tambourine. When they hear the sound of their musical instrument the team can move across the room. When the sound stops they must stand still. Make the sounds out of sight, alternating the instruments. The winner is the team that gets across the room first. (Give the teams different movements to carry out, such as skipping, hopping or walking backwards.)

Everyday routines

Use different sounds to signal different activities: for example, a bell for lunch, a whistle for the end of outside play.

Sound lotto

Sounds from musical instruments are recorded on audio tape. Pictures of the instruments are presented in the form of a lotto card. The child has to place a counter on the picture that matches the appropriate sound on the tape.

Giant picture lotto

Make a giant picture lotto. Pictures of musical instruments are drawn in the different squares on the lotto. Use real instruments to make the sounds. When a child hears a sound, she has to place a matching picture on the correct square. At the end the children can choose to hear different instruments by selecting pictures from the lotto.

SECTION 5

ACTIVITIES FOR
Home

Your child will learn to recognize musical instruments by listening to and copying sounds. Do not worry about asking her the names of the instruments at this stage. At first let your child watch as you make the sound with the objects. Later you can hide the objects behind the sofa or a large piece of card, so your child is relying on her listening skills alone.

☐ *Match a sound*

You will need two matching musical instruments or musical toys. (Home-made instruments can be used.) Make sure you and your child have one set of instruments each. Show the child how you can make a sound with one of the instruments. Encourage her to copy you with her matching instrument. Later you can hide your instruments. Can she copy the sound by listening alone? When she is familiar with the game, start to introduce more instruments.

☐ *Dancing*

Teach your child to do simple dances to different musical sounds. She could march like a soldier to the beat of a drum or tip-toe like a fairy to the sound of wind chimes. See if she can remember the dances if you play the instruments out of sight.

☐ *Music on the radio or television*

Draw your child's attention to the different musical instruments used in her favourite radio or television programmes.

Sounds &
SOUNDMAKERS

You may carry out sound recognition activities with a variety of musical instruments or music makers such as the following:

- ☐ cymbals
- ☐ maracas
- ☐ drum
- ☐ shakers
- ☐ wood blocks and mallet
- ☐ jingle bells
- ☐ triangles
- ☐ castanets
- ☐ tone blocks

- ☐ tambourines
- ☐ glockenspiel
- ☐ pali blocks and mallet
- ☐ shekere
- ☐ wooden agogo
- ☐ Tibetan bells
- ☐ tabla
- ☐ mouth organ
- ☐ recorder

Home-made musical instruments:

- ☐ wind chimes
- ☐ musical mobile
- ☐ empty biscuit tin and a wooden spoon (drum)
- ☐ frying pan or saucepan lid (gong)
- ☐ rattle
- ☐ toy piano

- ☐ silver foil bottle tops threaded on string
- ☐ empty bottles to blow into
- ☐ two sticks to tap together
- ☐ flower pot and stick to tap together

Talk to your child's speech and language therapist/clinician or teacher about the musical instruments that interest you and your child. Ask them to tick appropriate instruments from the above list.

SECTION 5

Everyday Objects
TEACHING ACTIVITY
'Guess the Object'

You will need:

two identical sets
of soundmaking
everyday objects – two
bunches of keys;
two spoons; two cups
(stir spoon in cup to
make a noise);
a screen.

**Useful words
and phrases:**

listen; look;
sound; wait; point;
name of objects; hide.

1 This activity can be carried out at a table or on the floor.

2 Introduce each object to the child by naming it and making a sound. Allow the child a few moments to explore the object. (For some children with poor attention skills it would be better to put one object away before showing another one.)

3 Place one set of the everyday objects in front of the child. They should be within easy reach of the child but not so close that they are tempted to pick them up.

4 Show the child that you have matching objects. Place your duplicate set near to you but still in sight of the child.

5 Ask the child to look and listen. Choose one object from your duplicate set and make a sound in her sight. Ask the child to find the matching object from her set.

6 If she is unsure or makes an incorrect choice, hold your object close to the duplicate one in her set. Give her your object to make a sound. Then repeat the task with the same object.

7 Continue until the child is consistently matching the objects by watching and listening.

8 Hide your objects behind a screen. Make a sound for several seconds and ask the child to find the matching object from her duplicate set.

9 If the child is unsuccessful on the first attempt, repeat the sound exactly. If she is still unsure or chooses incorrectly, make the sound in her sight.

10 Allow the child to play briefly with the object when she has made the correct choice.

To increase the complexity of the activity:

◆ increase the number of objects (seven to eight maximum);
◆ introduce objects that sound increasingly similar;
◆ ask the child to identify more than one object at a time (three maximum);
◆ use less familiar objects;
◆ introduce a delay before the child is allowed to respond.

Variations

◆ Vary the objects.

◆ Make a 'surprise box' by placing the objects in a suitcase. The child must open the suitcase and find the matching object. If you play this game with a group of children, this will stop them from helping each other by pointing. It also adds a natural delay.

◆ More able children can be asked to name the object.

◆ In a group game the children can take it in turns to make the sounds for the others.

Everyday Objects
ACTIVITIES FOR
School or Nursery

At first let the children see you make the sounds. Later you can hide the soundmakers so the children are relying on their listening skills alone. These activities help the child to recognize sounds made by everyday objects.

☐ Matching object to sound

Use two or three everyday objects which have matching pictures. (Use large flashcards and real objects.) Make a sound with one of the objects. Can the child point to the appropriate picture? Hide the objects behind a screen. Can she find the correct picture by listening to the sound alone?

☐ Giant picture lotto

Make a giant picture lotto. Draw pictures of different soundmaking objects in the different squares on the lotto. Use real everyday objects to make the sounds. When the child hears a sound she has to place a matching picture on the correct square. At the end the children can choose to hear different sounds by selecting object pictures from the lotto.

☐ Sound shakers

Place small objects, such as safety pins or buttons, in opaque shakers. Let the child see the objects being placed in the shakers and then listen to the sound they make. Mix up the containers. Make a sound with one of the shakers. Can the child identify the object from the sound? Have some duplicate objects in a transparent container for the child to indicate which objects made the sound.

☐ Sound lotto

Sounds from everyday objects are recorded on audio tape. Pictures of the objects are presented in the form of a lotto card. The child has to place a counter on the picture that matches the appropriate sound on the tape.

P

Everyday Objects
ACTIVITIES FOR
Home

These activities will help your child to recognize the sound made by everyday objects. Do not worry at this stage about your child naming the objects. At first let your child watch as you make the sound with the objects. Later you can hide the objects behind the sofa or a large piece of card, so your child is relying on her listening skills alone.

☐ *Match my object*

You will need some everyday objects. These could be buttons in a box and a spoon in a cup. Make sure you and your child have one each of the everyday objects. Show the child how you can make a sound with one of the objects. Encourage her to copy you. At first she may need to make sounds along with you. Later you can hide the objects. Can she copy the sounds by listening alone? Try this game using a variety of everyday objects.

☐ *Around the house*

Tap an object in the room. Use a wooden spoon or stick. (Be careful – do not hit your best china!) Can your child tap the same object? Ask her to close her eyes while you go around the room tapping objects. Can she still tap the same objects as you just by hearing the sound?

73

Sounds &
SOUNDMAKERS

You may carry out sound recognition activities with a variety of everyday objects such as the following;

- [ ] keys
- [ ] coins
- [ ] spoon in a cup or glass
- [ ] book shutting or dropping
- [ ] scrunchy paper
- [ ] scissors cutting paper
- [ ] pencil being sharpened
- [ ] water being poured
- [ ] knife scraping on a plate
- [ ] pencil scribbling
- [ ] fingers tapping on a table or window
- [ ] door banging

The following items can be placed in shakers:

- [ ] toy plastic animals
- [ ] small toys
- [ ] model vehicles
- [ ] safety pins
- [ ] paper clips
- [ ] keys
- [ ] coins
- [ ] beads

- [ ] matches (spent)
- [ ] paper strips
- [ ] pegs
- [ ] curtain hooks
- [ ] expanded polystyrene
- [ ] pebbles or stones
- [ ] cotton reels

P

! **Always be extremely careful with small objects which may be swallowed accidentally by young children. Items should be placed in shakers with** *secure* **lids. If in any doubt, use larger objects or toys. Specialist children's stores, such as Mothercare, sell a device for checking whether objects are small enough to be swallowed.**

Talk to your child's speech and language therapist/clinician or teacher about the everyday objects that interest you and your child. Ask them to tick appropriate objects from the above list.

SECTION 5

Everyday Sounds at Home
TEACHING ACTIVITY
'Sounds at Home'

You will need:

a tape recorder; an audio tape of two real noises recorded in the home (for example, a phone, and a vacuum cleaner); clear pictures of a phone and a vacuum cleaner (Winslow's *Indoor Sounds ColorCards* may be useful).

Useful words and phrases:

listen; look; tape; tape recorder; home; vacuum cleaner; telephone.

1 This activity can be carried out on the floor or at a table.

2 Introduce the pictures to the child. Name the items and ask the child about similar items in her own home. Place the pictures in view of the child.

3 During this activity it is acceptable for the child to join in with making the sounds or naming items and this can be reinforced by the adult through repetition. However responses should not be forced from the child.

4 Explain to the child that she will be listening to a tape with sounds she hears at home. Let the child see the tape recorder and if appropriate allow her to place the tape in the machine and switch it on.

5 Before playing the tape, check she is ready and listening.

6 Select the appropriate picture and play the first sound. Tell the child, "The phone is ringing." Play the same sound again for the child to hear as she looks at the picture.

7 Repeat this procedure with the other sound.

8 When both sounds have been demonstrated, play the first sound again. Ask the child which one makes that noise as you point to the pictures.

9 If the child is unsure or fails to make the correct response, play the sound again. Select the picture for the child if this fails to elicit the correct response.

10 After she has identified the picture correctly, let the child hear the sound again. This will reward and reinforce her learning.

To increase the complexity of the activity:

◆ gradually increase the number of home sounds
  (seven to eight maximum);
◆ introduce items that sound increasingly similar;
◆ ask the child to identify more than one home
  sound at a time (three maximum);
◆ use less familiar sounds;
◆ introduce a delay before the child is allowed to respond.

Variations

◆ Vary the sounds.
◆ Use toy objects that the child can use in 'pretend' play
  when she hears the sound on the tape.

ACTIVITIES FOR
School or Nursery

These activities help the child to recognize everyday sounds and soundmakers heard in the home. The children can show their understanding by pointing at pictures or selecting objects. They do not have to name the sounds or soundmakers.

☐ Sound lotto

Sounds from home are recorded on audio tape. Pictures that represent these sounds are presented in the form of a lotto card. The child has to place a counter on the picture that matches the appropriate sound on the tape. Sounds could include those made by the vacuum cleaner, telephone, and so on.

☐ Matching object to picture

Record several everyday sounds on a tape. The child has to match an object with a picture when she hears the appropriate sound. (Use large flashcards and miniature objects: for example, a toy telephone with a picture of a telephone.)

☐ Doll play

You will need a doll's house and two or three miniature items found in the home that make a noise, such as an alarm clock, a television and a radio. Record the sounds that these items make. Ask the child to place the miniature items in the doll's house when she hears the sound on the tape.

☐ 'Busy' pictures

Record different sounds heard in the home. Use a picture that illustrates the different items that make the sounds. For example, a picture of a kitchen might have a washing machine, a kettle boiling and water running. Ask the child to point to items in the picture when she hears the matching sound.

☐ Mime

Show the child how to mime using different soundmaking objects in the home. Each time she hears the sound she must mime using the object; for example, telephone – mime holding the receiver; vacuum cleaner – mime vacuuming the carpet.

P

Everyday Sounds at Home
ACTIVITIES FOR
Home

These activities will help the child to recognize different sounds and soundmakers around the home.

☐ *What made that sound?*

Draw your child's attention to sounds like the doorbell or the phone. Encourage her to help you answer the door or pick up the telephone. If she confuses two sounds, show her what is making the sound. Repeat the sound for her if you can, for example by ringing the doorbell again.

☐ *Walk round the home*

Ask your child to listen for a particular sound or sounds as you walk round your home. Your child could listen for the ticking of the alarm clock in the bedroom, the whirr of the fridge in the kitchen and the post coming through the door in the hall. Talk about the sounds you hear.

☐ *In the garden*

Listen for different sounds around the garden. Can your child hear sounds from next door? What are they?

Sounds &
SOUNDMAKERS

You may carry out sound recognition activities with a variety of everyday sounds. Some objects or events are better represented in picture form.

- ☐ telephone
- ☐ alarm clock
- ☐ radio
- ☐ tape recorder
- ☐ music box
- ☐ door knocker or bell
- ☐ vacuum cleaner
- ☐ washing machine
- ☐ toilet flushing

- ☐ cooking sounds
- ☐ footsteps
- ☐ pet noises (barking, miaowing)
- ☐ doors banging
- ☐ cleaning sounds (sweeping, rubbing)
- ☐ lawnmower
- ☐ clipper for hedge
- ☐ drill or hammer

Talk to your child's speech and language therapist/clinician or teacher about the soundmakers or sounds that interest you and your child. Ask them to tick appropriate soundmakers or sounds from the above list.

Human Sounds
TEACHING ACTIVITY
'Listen to Dolly'

1 Show the doll to the child. Explain that you will be playing a listening game with dolly.

2 Introduce the tissues to the child and talk about how they are used.

3 Make an exaggerated sneeze and tell the child that dolly needs her nose wiped.

4 Once the child has the idea that she must wipe dolly's nose when dolly (or rather you!) sneezes, you can introduce the medicine bottle and spoon. (For some children with poor attention skills, it would be better to put away the tissues first.)

5 Make an exaggerated cough and tell her to give dolly a spoonful of medicine.

6 When the child is confident with steps three to five, you can place all the items on the table within reach of the child. Make the sound of a sneeze or a cough. If the child does not respond, or chooses incorrectly, repeat the sound. It may be necessary to point to the correct item.

7 Continue until the child is responding consistently.

8 Cover your face with the screen and make a sneezing or coughing noise. Be careful not to give any clues by moving your head and so on.

9 If the child does not respond correctly, let her see you as you repeat the sound.

10 During the activity it is acceptable for the child to join in with making the sounds or naming items and this can be reinforced by the adult through repetition. However responses should not be forced from the child.

11 When the child chooses correctly, repeat the sound and indicate to the child that she is correct.

You will need:

a doll; tissues; a spoon; an empty medicine bottle; a screen (a screen can be made by placing opaque material in an embroidery frame).

Useful words and phrases:

look; listen; sneeze; wipe; cold; tissue; dolly; nose; cough; spoon; medicine; give.

To increase the complexity of the activity:

◆ gradually increase the number of noises (seven to eight maximum);

◆ introduce noises that sound increasingly similar;

◆ ask the child to identify more than one human sound at a time (three maximum);

◆ use less familiar human sounds;

◆ introduce a delay before the child is allowed to respond.

Variations

◆ Ask the child to respond in different ways, such as saying "Bless you" or patting dolly on the back.

◆ Record some sounds on a tape.

◆ Let the child have a turn at making the noises.

◆ Use other human sounds and appropriate actions.

Human Sounds
ACTIVITIES FOR
School or Nursery

These activities will help the child to recognize sounds made by humans, such as coughing and laughing.

☐ ### *Sound lotto*

Human sounds are recorded on audio tape. Pictures representing the sounds are presented in the form of a lotto card. The child has to place a counter on the picture that matches the appropriate sound on the tape. (Winslow's *Indoor Sounds ColorCards* may be useful.)

☐ ### *Giant picture lotto*

Make a giant picture lotto. Draw pictures that represent a variety of human sounds in the different squares on the lotto. Sounds can be recorded on a tape or made by an adult. When a child hears a sound she has to place a matching picture on the correct square. At the end the children can choose to hear different sounds by selecting pictures from the lotto.

☐ ### *How do they feel?*

Record human sounds that represent different emotions, such as crying or shouting. Have pictures of people showing different emotions, for example, sadness, happiness or anger, that match the sounds on the tape. Play a sound and ask the children to find the picture that goes with it. Talk about what made them choose that particular picture. Ask the children what sounds they make when they feel happy or excited.

ACTIVITIES FOR
Home

These activities help your child to learn about the sounds that are made by humans, such as laughing or coughing. Help your child by letting her see your face as you make a sound. Later she can play the games by listening alone.

☐ *Coughs and colds*

Ask your child to carry out actions with her doll when you make a sound. Suitable sounds and actions include blowing dolly's nose after she sneezes or patting her back when she coughs.

☐ *'Ring-a-Ring-of-Roses'*

Sing this song with your child. Leave pauses for her to fill in the sneezes. Give her a clue by holding your nose.

☐ *Picture books*

Look at pictures of people who are happy, sad or angry. Talk about the sounds that people make when they have different feelings. Ask your child to mime the different emotions using facial expression, body posture and sounds.

Sounds & SOUNDMAKERS

You may carry out sound recognition activities with a variety of human noises such as the following:

- ☐ laughter
- ☐ crying
- ☐ shouting
- ☐ talking
- ☐ voices expressing different emotions
- ☐ yawning
- ☐ sneezing
- ☐ coughing
- ☐ moan of pain

Talk to your child's speech and language therapist/clinician or teacher about the sounds that interest you and your child. Ask them to tick appropriate sounds from the above list.

Animal Sounds
TEACHING ACTIVITY
'Animal Puppets'

You will need:

two pairs of animal puppets (for example, a cat and a dog); a large opaque bag.

Useful words and phrases:

listen; look; animal names; animal noises; bag.

1 This activity can be carried out on the floor or at a table.

2 Introduce one set of puppets to the child. Allow the child to try on each puppet and to stroke its fur. Name the animals and ask the child about her own pets. Place the puppets in view of the child.

3 Tell the child you have some more animals hidden in the bag. She must listen carefully for the sound of the animal.

4 Put your hand in the bag and put on one of the puppets. Make the appropriate noise for several seconds.

5 Ask the child to show you which animal is making the noise.

6 If the child fails to make the correct response, repeat the sound. It may be necessary to cue the child by pointing to the puppet on the table or imitating some of the characteristics of the animal; for example, a cat may lick her paw. Select the animal puppet for the child if this fails to elicit the correct response.

7 During the activity it is acceptable for the child to join in with making the sounds or naming the animals and this can be reinforced by the adult through repetition. However responses should not be forced from the child.

8 When the animal has been correctly identified bring out the matching puppet from the bag and make the noise again.

9 Let the child try on the puppet and make the noise. This will reward and reinforce the child's learning.

To increase the complexity of the activity:

◆ gradually increase the number of animal sounds
(seven to eight maximum);

◆ introduce animal noises that sound increasingly similar;

◆ ask the child to identify more than one animal sound at a
time (three maximum);

◆ use less familiar animal sounds;

◆ introduce a delay before the child responds.

Variations

◆ Vary the animals and animal sounds.

◆ Use miniature toys instead of puppets.

◆ Record some sounds on a tape (or use Winslow's *Outdoor
Sounds ColorCards*).

◆ Let the child have a turn at making the noises.

Animal Sounds

ACTIVITIES FOR
School or Nursery

These activities will help the child to recognize different animal sounds. At first let the children watch your face as you make the animal sound. Later you can hide your face with a large card or use recorded sounds so that the children are relying on their listening skills alone.

☐ Lost animals

You will need several animal puppets. Explain to the children that they are going to be zoo keepers and that several animals have escaped. Their job is to round up the lost animals and collect them in the bag for return to the zoo. Hide several animal puppets around the room and tell the children to listen very carefully. When the child hears a sound she must find the animal that is making the noise. (Make the sounds near to the children and not the animal puppets. Otherwise the children will have to locate the sound as well as identify it.) If the child is incorrect, the animal is released again. (You could also try lost animals with a farmer, circus ringmaster or pet shop owner.)

☐ Find the matching picture

You will need several animal pictures with matching miniature animals. Place the pictures on a table with the miniatures to one side. Ask each child to place the miniature animal on the matching picture when she hears the appropriate sound. (Sounds can be recorded or imitated by an adult.)

☐ Sound lotto

Sounds from animals are recorded on audio tape. Pictures of the animals are presented in the form of a lotto card. The child has to place a counter on the picture that matches the appropriate sound on the tape. Winslow's *Outdoor Sounds ColorCards* may be useful.

Giant picture lotto

Make a giant picture lotto. Draw pictures of animals in the different squares on the lotto. Record the animal sounds on tape. When a child hears a sound, she has to place a matching picture on the correct square. At the end the children can choose to hear different animal sounds by selecting pictures from the lotto. (You may find Winslow's *Outdoor Sounds ColorCards* useful.)

Animal silhouettes

Use several plastic animal shapes. Ask the child to draw around the shape when she hears the animal sound. She can colour in the picture to make the animal silhouettes.

Animal Sounds
ACTIVITIES FOR
Home

Your child will learn to recognize animal sounds by listening to and copying sounds. At first let your child watch your face as you make the animal sound. Later you can cover your mouth with your hand so that your child is just listening.

☐ *'Old MacDonald had a Farm'*

Sing this song. Encourage your child to join in with the animal sounds. Show your child pictures of the animals when you make the sounds. Can your child point to the appropriate picture when you make the sound?

☐ *'Baa Baa Black Sheep'*

Teach your child this rhyme. Encourage her to join in with the sheep sounds. Do you know any other rhymes with animal sounds?

☐ *Animal stories*

Look at animal picture books. Make a sound and ask your child to find the animal. She can make sounds for you to find the picture.

☐ *Mime this animal*

Talk about animals your child has seen in books or at the zoo. Make the animal noises while you mime appropriate actions. You could:

☐ miaow and pretend to lick a paw;

☐ bark and pant like a dog;

☐ roar and make your hands like the claws of a tiger;

☐ say, "oink oink" and snort like a pig;

☐ say, "quack quack" and make your hand like a beak;

☐ moo and pretend to chew grass.

Make a sound. Can your child mime the animal?

Pets on tape

Help your child to record the sounds of her pets. Make the sound of one of her pets. Can she find it on the tape?

Animal masks

Help your child to make a large colourful animal mask out of card and string. Make sure the mask has holes for the eyes and nose. Encourage your child to make animal sounds. Wear a mask yourself and make some sounds.

I am a...

Paint an animal face on your child. (Special face paints can be bought from toy shops.) Encourage your child to make the sound of the animal.

Sounds &
SOUNDMAKERS

Animals can be represented by a variety of toys and other items:

- ☐ cuddly animal toys
- ☐ plastic animal shapes
- ☐ pictures or photographs of animals
- ☐ miniature animals
- ☐ animal masks

Here are some commercial listening games with animal sounds:

- ☐ 'Animal Sounds', DLM/Taskmaster
- ☐ 'Photo Sound Lotto (Animals)', LDA
- ☐ 'Look Hear (Animals)', LDA
- ☐ *Outdoor Sounds ColorCards*, Winslow

The following is a list of animal sounds that can be used in sound recognition games:

- ☐ cat – miaow
- ☐ dog – woof woof
- ☐ cow – moo
- ☐ pig – oink
- ☐ duck – quack

- ☐ horse – neigh
- ☐ sheep – baa
- ☐ chicken – cluck
- ☐ cockerel – cock-a-doodle-doo
- ☐ bear – growl

- ☐ monkey – oo-oo
- ☐ lion – roar
- ☐ bee – buzz
- ☐ bird – whistle or cheep

Talk to your child's speech and language therapist/clinician or teacher about the sounds and materials that interest you and your child. Ask them to tick appropriate sounds and materials from the above list.

Sound Recognition
CHECKLIST

Child's name	

Date	Activity	Comments
Example **23.2.**	*Everyday sounds*	*Picks up telephone when it rings.*

FINDING SOUND

SECTION 6

INTRODUCTION

THIS SECTION contains activities designed to develop the child's ability to localize sound. Sound location is important in the development of listening skills such as sound discrimination and sound recognition. In addition, the ability to localize sound will help the child identify speakers, enabling her to respond appropriately to others and engage in conversations.

Sound location is vital not only for the child's language development but also for basic safety reasons. For example, when we cross the road we are partly looking for cars and partly listening. A car approaching us from behind will be heard before it is seen.

Children with a hearing loss are likely to have difficulties with localizing sound but these activities are also useful for developing early listening skills in children with communication problems. They can be modified for those children who can detect sound but are unable to identify it. They will also help the child's concentration and memory for sound.

It is important that sounds are presented at the appropriate distance, height and angle to the child. The guidelines give advice on how to present sounds in the activities. This is based on the developmental stages of sound location in the young infant and the auditory needs of children with a hearing loss. Remember that some children may be responding to other cues in localization activities – they may see your shadow or smell your scent.

Be aware of physical difficulties that prevent the child from turning to locate the sound, such as poor head control. Seek the advice of a physiotherapist on supporting the child's posture.

It is particularly important in sound localization that parents are given careful advice on how to carry out the activities. Use the 'Hints for Parents' sheet (p99) to record information for the parent.

GUIDELINES FOR
Finding Sound

The sound source should be at a distance from the child of one metre or less when she is beginning to learn sound localization. This distance can be increased as the child's skills develop. The position of the soundmaker is also important. The child will respond first to sounds made at the side and level with the ear.

Decide at what height and angle you will present the sounds to the child. Use the hierarchy below, which is based on the developmental stages of sound location in the young infant.

at the side and level with the right ear;

at the side and level with the left ear;

at the side and level with the ear on either side;

at the side and below the right ear;

at the side and below the left ear;

at the side and above the right ear;

at the side and above the left ear;

at any angle to the ear (that is behind, to the side or in front of the ear).

HINTS FOR PARENTS

Ask your speech and language therapist or teacher about the following:

◆ how far from your child to make the sound;

◆ where to hold the soundmaker: for example, next to her ear, behind her;

◆ who can help your child if she has physical difficulties which prevent her from turning to find the sound.

Ask your child's speech and language therapist/clinician or teacher to fill this in for you.

Make the sounds for your child:

☐ at the same height as your child's ear

☐ at the side of your child

☐ behind your child

☐ above the child's ear

☐ below the child's ear

☐ at .... distance

Remember that your child may be using other cues to find the sound. She may see your shadow or smell your scent.

Musical Instruments
TEACHING ACTIVITY
'Point to the Sound'

This activity is designed for three children but it can be played with one child and two adults. Place three chairs in a row so that the two outer chairs face the middle in at right angles (see illustration). There should be approximately one metre of space between each chair. Make sure that the seating arrangement allows sounds to be presented at ear level.

You will need:

two identical shakers; three chairs of the same height.

Useful words and phrases:

listen; look; close your eyes; where is the sound?; who made the sound?; right; left; middle; point; make a noise.

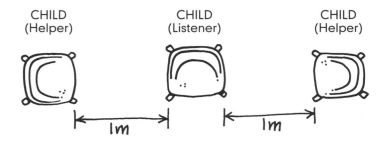

CHILD (Helper)   CHILD (Listener)   CHILD (Helper)

1m   1m

1. Sit one child in the middle. Two other children should take up positions as helpers at the side of her.

2. Give each helper at the side a shaker to hold.

3. Explain to the child in the middle that a sound will be made which might come from her right ear or her left. (Use the names of the children if this is easier for the child.)

4. Indicate to one of the helpers at the side that they should make a noise with the shaker. (Use pointing or some other agreed signal.)

5. Ask the child in the middle to point to the one who made the sound.

6. Once the child is familiar with the task and is consistently pointing to the sound, ask her to close her eyes and then repeat the activity. A blindfold can be used if she is agreeable.

7. If the child makes a mistake, ask her to look while the sound is repeated.

8. When the child is correct, she must be praised so that she is clear about her success and be allowed to see who has made the sound.

P

To increase the complexity of the activity:

◆ make the sound of the shaker quieter;

◆ increase the distance between the child and the shaker;

◆ use fewer repetitions of the sound;

◆ gradually change the angle of the shaker to the child (*see* guidelines on pp98-9).

Variations

◆ Some children may find this activity easier if they only have to respond by *turning* towards the sound. An adult distracts the child at the front (for example, by showing her pictures or blowing bubbles), while another helper stands behind and makes the sounds. Remember to stop the distraction before the sound is made, otherwise the child may be too engrossed to hear it.

◆ Vary the musical instruments used.

◆ Give each child at the side an empty shoe box which has one side cut out so the shaker can be hidden away. This way, the other child can keep her eyes open.

These activities will help the child in locating sound. Games using musical instruments are more fun for the child and do not require her to understand or use language.

☐ *Find the musical instrument*

Sit one child in the middle of a small circle of children and give her a picture of a musical instrument. She closes her eyes or is blindfolded while the children pass the instrument around the group. At a signal from you the children stop and the child holding the instrument uses it to make a noise and then hides it. The listener in the middle must give the picture to the child she thinks has made the noise. (Make sure the children are well spaced out for this activity.)

☐ *Who has the bell?*

Sit one child in the middle of a small circle of children. She closes her eyes while you give one child a bell, small enough to hide in her hand. (A bell for a bird cage would be about the right size.) Tell the children in the circle to shake their clenched hands in the air. The child in the middle is asked to open her eyes and point to the one who has the bell. (Make sure the children are well spaced out for this activity.)

☐ *Symbols*

Older children can play this game. Draw three symbols on a chart, for example, three circles in a row. Place a counter on the middle symbol. Seat two children so that they are on either side of the child but out of her sight. They take it in turns to make a sound using a musical instrument. (Make sure they avoid a pattern, such as right, left, right, left, otherwise the child in the middle will be able to anticipate the direction of the sound.) The child in the middle moves the counter to the symbol on the right or left, depending on the direction of the sound.

Sound in stories

Select a story which provides plenty of opportunity for using a musical instrument. A story about guests arriving for a party might have a bell or 'Three Little Pigs' might have a drum to represent the wolf knocking on the door. (You might like to use several different instruments.) Tell the story to the children and make the different sounds when appropriate.

Give out several instruments to the children. This time the children make the sounds as you tell the story. You can cue the children by pointing to them when it is their turn to make a sound. Practise until all the children are familiar with the story and know when to make the sounds.

Seat the children in a circle. Choose one child to sit as the listener in the middle of the circle. Explain to her that you will tell the story and when she hears a sound she must point to the child who she thinks made the sound. Ask her to close her eyes or wear a blindfold. Tell the story and help each child to make a sound in the right place. The listener can collect the instruments each time she is correct. (Make sure the children are well spaced out for this activity.)

Think of a story

Repeat the 'Sound in stories' activity, but this time help the children to make up their own story. Let them choose the soundmakers.

Story teller

Repeat the 'Sound in stories' activity. Can the child in the middle tell the story, as well as listen for the sounds?

 Always be extremely cautious when carrying out activities where the child has her eyes closed or is blindfolded.

103

Musical Instruments
ACTIVITIES FOR
Home

These games will help your child to learn to locate sounds. Your child will enjoy listening for the musical instruments. Make sure the room is as quiet as possible.

☐ *Roll a sound*

Use a toy that makes a musical sound when it is rolled along the ground. Play with your child rolling the toy between you. She can follow the toy by watching and listening.

☐ *Who's that?*

Play this game with another adult whom the child likes. Both adults should have a musical toy, such as a rattle or mouth organ. Sit on one side of your child; the other person should sit on the other side. Take it in turns to make a sound. When your child turns to the sound, let her play with the toy.

☐ *Turn to the sound*

Play this game with your child, using a rattle, shaker or other musical instrument. Stand behind her and make a sound with the musical instrument. Does she turn to the sound? At first she may need prompting. You could call her name and make the sound again when she turns.

   Perhaps another child or adult could be a helper. They should sit in front of the child and prompt her to turn. They can also keep your child's attention and stop her from turning before you make the sound.

☐ *Hide the music*

Play hiding games with your child. Use a musical instrument like a drum or rattle and hide somewhere in the room. Make a sound. Can your child find you by listening for the sound?

Where's the music box?

Hide a music box in the room. Can your child find it by listening for the sound? Use a music box that only plays for a short time. Your child will have to be quick to find the box before the music stops.

'Squeak, Piggy, Squeak'

Play this game at a party. One blindfolded child sits in the middle of a small circle of children, while another child from the circle is chosen to be the 'piggy' and is given a squeaker. The 'piggy' must wait for the child in the middle to call out "Squeak, piggy, squeak" before she makes the noise. If the child in the middle is successful at pointing to 'piggy' they swap places. (Make sure the children are well spaced out for this activity.)

 Always be extremely cautious when carrying out activities where the child has her eyes closed or is blindfolded.

Sounds &
SOUNDMAKERS

Try using a variety of musical instruments or music makers to play finding sound games. Choose ones that have a longer vibration time or the duration of whose sound can be extended, such as:

- ☐ record player
- ☐ radio
- ☐ cassette player
- ☐ chime bars
- ☐ jingle bells
- ☐ bells on sticks
- ☐ hand-held bells
- ☐ music box

- ☐ squeaker
- ☐ tambourine
- ☐ sonar resonator tone bars (these are good resonators for the deaf and hard of hearing)
- ☐ tulip block
- ☐ cabasa afuche
- ☐ Tibetan bells

Home-made musical instruments:

- ☐ empty biscuit tin and a wooden spoon (drum)
- ☐ frying pan or saucepan lid (gong)
- ☐ rattle
- ☐ silver foil bottle tops threaded on string
- ☐ two sticks to tap together
- ☐ flower pot and stick to tap together

Talk to your child's speech and language therapist/clinician or teacher about the musical instruments that interest you and your child. Ask them to tick appropriate instruments from the above list.

Animal Sounds
TEACHING ACTIVITY
'Farmer Find Your Animals'

1 Seat the children in a circle on the floor or on chairs. Explain that they are going to be playing a listening game. (It is important that the children are able to recognize animal sounds, as well as being able to make sounds, before they try this activity. You may like to spend some time practising this before you start.)

2 Choose one child as the farmer and ask her to stand in the middle of the circle and close her eyes. (She can wear a blindfold if she is agreeable, or you could ask all the children in the outer circle to put their heads down so their faces are hidden.)

3 One child in the circle is chosen to be an animal, such as a cow. Let the group decide which animal.

4 She must wait for the child in the centre to say, "Where are you, cow?" before she makes a noise.

5 The farmer in the middle must point to where the noise is coming from.

6 If the farmer is unsure, let her see the location of the sound.

7 When the animal is found she joins the farmer in the middle.

8 The game continues with a different child until all the animals are collected by the farmer.

To increase the complexity of the activity:
◆ ask the child to make the animal sound quieter;
◆ increase the distance between the animal and the farmer;
◆ have fewer repetitions of the animal sounds.

You will need:

a large floor space where the children can sit in a circle.

Useful words and phrases:

*listen; look;
name of the animal;
farmer;
where is the...?*

S E C T I O N **6**

Variations

◆ The child in the circle chooses an animal sound to make, but does not tell anyone the animal. The 'farmer' has to guess the animal as well as point to the sound. (Remember that the child must be at the stage to recognize animal sounds.)

◆ The farmer is given a picture of an animal. When she hears the sound of the animal she must give the picture to the child she thinks is making the sound.

◆ Give the farmer a picture of an animal; this time two or three different animal sounds are made. The farmer must wait till she hears the sound of the animal in the picture before she points to the sound. (The children should be familiar with the teaching activity before attempting this game.)

Animal Sounds
ACTIVITIES FOR
School or Nursery

These activities help the children to develop skills in locating sound. They will enjoy the animal theme.

☐ *Dangerous animals*

Sit one child on a chair. On either side of her, behind screens, are two other children. Explain to the children that the screens are rocks and a dangerous animal might be hiding behind them. (Be careful that the screens are not so thick that they muffle the sound.) Tell the child seated in the middle to listen very carefully. If she hears the sound of an animal she must point to where she thinks it is hiding. Signal to one of the children behind the rocks to make a sound. If the child points at the correct rock the child who is hiding can leap out and make a frightening animal noise.

☐ *Lost animals*

One child is chosen to pretend to be a lost animal. She moves quietly round the room crying plaintively every now and then. How long is it before the blindfolded 'owner' can find her by pointing to the sound?

☐ *'Lost Kitty'*

Play 'Lost Kitty'. One child closes her eyes while another child is chosen as the kitten and hides somewhere in the room. The first child opens her eyes and calls for the 'kitten', who miaows loudly until she is found.

☐ *Here, chick chick!*

You will need several blank pictures, two or three pictures of chicks and one picture of a hen. The children each select a picture without letting the other children see them. The child with the hen picture leaves the room. The other children form a circle, including the two or three children who have pictures of chicks. When the hen returns, all the children put their heads down. (This way the hen will not see who is making the noise.) The hen calls to her chicks with a cluck. The chicks reply with a chirp-chirp. The hen must point to those she thinks are the chicks.

Always be extremely cautious when carrying out activities where the child has her eyes closed or is blindfolded.

Animal Sounds
ACTIVITIES FOR
Home

These activities use animal sounds to help your child learn to locate sound. She will enjoy hearing and making the different sounds.

☐ *Hide-and-seek*

Pretend to be an animal. Hide somewhere in the room while your child closes her eyes. Make an animal sound. Can your child find you? Ask her to hide and make an animal noise for you to find her.

☐ *Animal faces*

Play hide-and-seek as above, but wear an animal face that matches the sound you are making. Jump out when your child finds you and mime the animal.

☐ *Farm or zoo visit*

At the farm or zoo talk to your child about the different animal sounds she can hear around her. As you walk around, draw her attention to the sounds of animals which you can hear but which are out of sight. Ask her to point to where she thinks they are. Go and see if she is right. Which animal does she think is the noisiest? The monkey house is usually pretty noisy.

☐ *Everyday animals*

Listen for animal sounds when you are walking with your child in the park or along the street. Tell her if you hear a dog barking or a cat miaowing. Ask her where the dog or cat is that made the sound.

 Always be extremely cautious when carrying out activities where the child has her eyes closed or is blindfolded.

Sounds &
SOUNDMAKERS

The following toys can be used to represent animal noises:

- ☐ cuddly animal toys
- ☐ plastic animal shapes
- ☐ pictures or photographs of animals
- ☐ animal masks
- ☐ miniature animals
- ☐ animal puppets

Animal sounds that can be used in the above activities are:

- ☐ cat – miaow
- ☐ dog – woof woof
- ☐ budgie – cheep, chirp
- ☐ parrot – squawk
- ☐ cow – moo
- ☐ pig – oink
- ☐ duck – quack

- ☐ horse – neigh
- ☐ sheep – baa
- ☐ chicken – cluck
- ☐ cockerel – cock-a-doodle-doo
- ☐ bear – growl
- ☐ monkey – oo-oo
- ☐ lion – roar

Talk to your child's speech and language therapist/clinician or teacher about the sounds and materials that interest you and your child. Ask them to tick appropriate sounds and materials from the above list.

Everyday Objects
TEACHING ACTIVITY
'Ticking Clock'

This activity is best carried out in a small room or in a partitioned part of a larger room. It should be quiet and free of clutter. However, there should be plenty of places where the clock can easily be hidden.

You will need:

a loudly ticking clock; two boxes large enough to hide the clock; a cloth.

Useful words and phrases:

look; listen; where's the clock?; close your eyes; ticking; hide; box.

1 Seat the child on the floor or on a chair, preferably in a corner where she has a good view of the room.

2 Show the boxes to the child.

3 Place them in sight of the child but about one metre apart.

4 Show the clock to the child. Cover it with a cloth and ask her to listen to the sound of the clock ticking. Explain that you are going to hide the clock in one of the two boxes.

5 Ask the child to close her eyes as you hide the clock.

6 When you are ready, ask her to open her eyes and stand by the boxes. Show her how to listen for the sound of the ticking. Encourage her to tell you which box has the hidden clock. Let her take the clock out when she finds the right box.

7 When the child is successful with this game let her have turns at finding the clock when you hide it around the room. (At this stage let her *watch*.)

8 Next ask her to close her eyes while you hide the clock in the room. (Remember to hide the clock at the child's ear level.)

9 When you are ready, ask the child to find the clock. If she has difficulty, lead her near to the clock.

When the child finds the clock, emphasize the sound of the ticking before the child brings it back.

To increase the complexity of the activity:

◆ use a clock with a quieter tick;

◆ ask the child to stand still and point to the sound;

◆ gradually increase the distance between the clock and the child;

◆ use an alarm clock, as the sound of the alarm will be shorter than the continuous ticking of the clock;

◆ hide the clock at different heights; that is, above and below ear level.

Variations

◆ Several clocks are placed around the room but only one is ticking. Ask the child to point to the clock she thinks is ticking. Let her go up and check her answers.

◆ Use other everyday objects that make a noise.

Everyday Objects
ACTIVITIES FOR
School or Nursery

Use everyday objects that make a sound to play these hiding games. It is important that the room is as quiet as possible and that any outside noise is kept to a minimum.

☐ *Symbols*

Older children can play this game. Draw three symbols on a chart, such as three circles in a row. Place a counter on the middle symbol. Seat two children so that they are on either side of the child but out of her sight. They take it in turns to make a sound using an everyday object. (Make sure they avoid a pattern, such as right, left, right, left, otherwise the child in the middle will be able to anticipate the direction of the sound.) The child in the middle moves the counter to the symbol on the right or left, depending on the direction of the sound.

☐ *Who has the object?*

Sit one child in the middle of a small circle of children. She closes her eyes while the other children pass an everyday object around the group. At a signal from you, the children stop and the child holding the object makes a noise and then hides it. The listener in the middle must point to the child she thinks has made the noise. (Make sure the children are well spaced out for this activity.)

☐ *Team games*

The children are divided into two teams, who take it in turns to find a ticking clock hidden in the room. Each team is timed to see which is the quicker to find the clock.

114
Early Listening Skills

© *Diana Williams 1995*
You may photocopy this page for instructional use only

P

Match the picture to the sound

Try this activity with those children who are able to recognize sounds. Have two or three pictures of everyday objects (Speechmark's *Everyday Objects ColorCards* may be useful). Hide in the room one object represented in the pictures. Ask one of the children to point to the sound. Before they find the object they must point to the picture of the object they think is making the sound.

Sound in stories

Select a well-known story which provides plenty of opportunity for using different sounds. Tell the story to the children and make the different sounds when appropriate.

Give out soundmakers to several of the children. This time the children make the sounds as you tell the story. You can cue the children by pointing to them when it is their turn to make a sound. Practise until all the children are familiar with the story and know when to make the sounds.

Seat the children in a circle. Choose one child to sit as the listener in the middle of the circle. Explain to her that you will tell the story and when she hears a sound she must point to the child who she thinks made the sound. Ask her to close her eyes. Tell the story and help each child to make a sound in the right place. The listener can collect the soundmaker each time she is correct. (Make sure the children are well spaced out for this activity.)

Always be extremely cautious when carrying out activities where the child has her eyes closed or is blindfolded.

115

Everyday Objects
ACTIVITIES FOR
Home

These are activities that use everyday objects in the home to help your child learn about locating sound. It is important that there is no background noise when you play these games.

☐ *Where is the sound?*

You will need two boxes and an everyday object that makes a loud noise, such as a ticking clock. Show your child the two empty boxes. Explain that you are going to hide the object in one of the boxes. Tell her to close her eyes. Put the object in one of the boxes and place it to one side of the child. Place the other box on the other side of her. Ask her to open her eyes and listen. Can she point to the box which has the sound?

☐ *Ticking clock*

Hide a ticking clock in the room. Can your child find it by listening for the tick-tock? Start with places near to the child and gradually increase the distance. Hide other soundmaking objects.

☐ *Pick a sound*

Hide two or three soundmaking objects around the room, such as an electronic key finder, a ticking clock and a music box. (Make sure the objects are well spaced out.) Ask your child to find one of the objects. Encourage her to walk around the room and listen carefully. (This is a particularly hard task as the child has to locate one sound among others. The room should be as quiet as possible.)

 Always be extremely cautious when carrying out activities where the child has her eyes closed or is blindfolded.

Sounds &
SOUNDMAKERS

Try these soundmakers:

- ☐ ticking clock
- ☐ radio
- ☐ electronic key finder
- ☐ music box
- ☐ alarm (anti-theft device etc)
- ☐ a metronome instead of a clock
- ☐ alarm clock
- ☐ cassette player

Talk to your child's speech and language therapist/clinician or teacher about the soundmakers that interest you and your child. Ask them to tick appropriate soundmakers from the above list.

Action Sounds
TEACHING ACTIVITY
'Don't Wake the Monster'

You will need:

a large floor space.

Useful words and phrases:

listen;
stand in the middle;
don't wake the monster!;
quietly;
where is the noise?

1 This activity is best when played with a group of children in a large, roomy area which is quiet and free from interruptions.

2 One child is chosen to be the 'monster'. Ask her to stand in the centre of the room wearing a blindfold, or with her eyes closed. The other children take up positions around the room, being careful to leave spaces between themselves.

3 One child is instructed to start moving around the room when the adult points at her. She must be as quiet as possible, so as not to wake the monster.

4 If she is able to get round the room without being caught by the monster, another child takes her place.

5 The child in the centre must listen very carefully for the sound of any movement. If she hears any movement she must point in the direction of the noise. (As children always find it difficult to keep quiet, the child will soon give herself away. Other children must be warned that they will be 'out' if they make a noise.)

6 If the child is unsure or makes a mistake, let her see where the noise is coming from. (Hold her hand so that she can compare where the sound is to where she pointed.)

7 If the child in the middle is correct, she swaps places with the other child, who then becomes the monster.

To increase the complexity of the activity:

◆ increase the distance between the child in the middle and the children around her.

Variations

◆ Children take it in turns to do an action, such as stamping their feet or clapping their hands. The child in the middle has to locate the sound and copy the action before they can swap places.

◆ The children are asked to wear something that makes a noise, such as bells around the ankles, or to walk on noisy paper.

P

Action Sounds

ACTIVITIES FOR
School or Nursery

These activities help the children with locating sound made at a distance. They are particularly suited for physical play. Remember to keep background noise to a minimum.

☐ *Don't wake the monster*

One child is chosen to be the 'monster' and is asked to stand in the centre of the room wearing a blindfold, or with her eyes closed. The other children take up positions around the room, being careful to leave spaces between themselves.

One child is instructed to start moving around the room when the adult points at her. She must be as quiet as possible, so as not to wake the monster. The child in the centre must listen very carefully for the sound of any movement. If she hears any movement she must point in the direction of the noise. (As children always find it difficult to keep quiet, the child will soon give herself away. The other children must be warned that they will be 'out' if they make a noise.)

If the child in the middle is correct, she swaps places with the other child, who then becomes the monster.

☐ *Find that action*

One child is chosen to stand in the centre of the room wearing a blindfold, or with her eyes closed. The other children take up positions around the room, being careful to leave spaces between themselves. The children take it in turns to do an action, such as stamping their feet or clapping their hands. The child in the middle has to locate the sound and copy the action. If she is right, she can swap places with the other child.

Sound obstacle course

You will need to set up a circular sound obstacle course. Place items in the course that will make it difficult for the child to be quiet: for example, rice paper, leaves or a tunnel to crawl through. (See other ideas on p122.) Split the children into teams. One child is asked to pass round the course. A child from the other team is chosen as the listener and must stand blindfolded in the middle of the course. She must try to catch the other child by pointing in the direction of any sounds she hears. (To stop any cheating, she must say what she has heard before she looks.) If she is right, the other child is 'out'. Continue with different pairs of children from the two teams. The winning team is the one with the most children who have passed through the course without being caught.

Party games

There are lots of party games that involve sound location. See below, 'Activities for Home', for suitable games.

 Always be extremely cautious when carrying out activities where the child has her eyes closed or is blindfolded.

Action Sounds

ACTIVITIES FOR
Home

There are lots of traditional party games that involve finding sound. Help your child by holding her hand when she has pointed to the sound. This way she can see how near her point was to the source of the sound. These games need to be played where there is plenty of space.

☐ *'Blind Man's Buff'*

One child is blindfolded. The other children move around. The blindfolded child tries to catch the other children by listening for any movements.

☐ *Grandmother's footsteps*

One child plays grandmother. She stands facing one wall. All the other children stand at the other side of the room. They must try to creep up and touch grandmother. If grandmother hears a sound she can turn round. Any child still moving is out of the game.

☐ *Dragon's treasure*

The children try to steal the dragon's treasure. Choose a child to be the dragon. She must sit blindfolded in the middle of the room. The other children must try to creep up and steal the treasure. If the dragon hears a sound she must point in the direction of the noise. Any child caught trying to steal the treasure is out of the game. (The treasure could be chocolate coins wrapped in gold paper. At the end of the game the children can eat them.) Instead of a dragon, you could have a king, queen, pirate or giant.

☐ *Catch the sound*

In this game all the children except one are blindfolded. The remaining child is given something noisy to wear, such as a cowbell on a necklace. She must walk quickly from one end of the room to the other without getting caught by the other children.

Always be extremely cautious when carrying out activities where the child has her eyes closed or is blindfolded.

Sounds &
SOUNDMAKERS

Action sounds include:

- [ ] clapping
- [ ] stamping feet
- [ ] running
- [ ] walking
- [ ] banging
- [ ] knocking

- [ ] hopping
- [ ] tapping foot
- [ ] sliding foot
- [ ] drumming fingers
- [ ] clicking fingers
- [ ] jumping

Ideas for a 'sound' obstacle course include:

- [ ] walking through dried leaves
- [ ] climbing through a hoop with bells or scrunchy paper tied around it
- [ ] crawling along a plastic tunnel
- [ ] jumping from one hoop (laid on the floor) to another
- [ ] carrying a bell
- [ ] carrying a box of marbles
- [ ] wearing noisy bracelets or anklets
- [ ] throwing coins onto cushions (there will be plenty of noise if one misses)
- [ ] blowing up a balloon
- [ ] crawling under a line hung with noisy paper

Talk to your child's speech and language therapist/clinician or teacher about the sounds and materials that interest you and your child. Ask them to tick appropriate sounds and materials from the above list.

Environmental Sounds
TEACHING ACTIVITY
'Stop and Listen'

(N.B. Children must have been successful at the previous teaching activities in this section before attempting this activity.)

1 Go to the middle of the school hall or main nursery corridor and tell the children to listen to the noises around them.

2 Talk about the noises they can hear.

3 Choose one of the children to listen. Ask her to close her eyes and tell you the first sound that she hears. Then ask her to point in the direction of the sound.

4 Keep her hand pointing in that direction by holding it, so that she can compare this with where the actual sound source is located. When she has located the sound, encourage her to close her eyes and listen again.

5 Continue until all the children have had a turn.

6 Next repeat the activity, but this time, when the child has her eyes closed or is blindfolded, spin her around to disorient her. (Warn her first!) So now, if the child recognizes a sound, such as saucepans banging, she will have to listen and not use her knowledge of the location of the kitchens.

7 Let her see where she has pointed and compare this with where the sound is located.

8 When she has localized the sound source, encourage her to close her eyes and listen again.

9 Continue until all the children have had a turn.

To increase the complexity of the activity:

◆ ask the children to locate sounds that are quiet or far away;
◆ choose environments that have less familiar sounds (for example, a zoo or a farm).

Variation

◆ Split the group into two teams. The winners are the team that has the most correct 'finds'.

You will need:

nothing; but access to a school hall or nursery corridor is desirable.

Useful words and phrases:

listen; look;
where is the sound?;
what do you hear?;
near; far;
point to the sound.

S E C T I O N 6

Environmental Sounds
ACTIVITIES FOR
School or Nursery

These activities encourage the children to think about the sounds they hear around them in their environment. They also help to develop the children's skills for locating sound sources.

☐ *Listen to the sounds*

Ask the children to close their eyes and listen to the sounds around them. Can they point in the direction of the sounds?

☐ *Find the sound*

Go into the hall or playground and repeat the above activity. Let the children take turns at locating different sounds. Ask the child to close her eyes and then spin her around to disorient her. (Warn her first!) This way, if the child recognizes a sound, such as saucepans banging, she will have to listen and not use her knowledge of the location of the kitchens.

☐ *Near and far games*

Ask the children to close their eyes and listen to the sounds around them. Can they tell you which sounds are near and which ones are far? Ask them to point to different near and far sounds.

☐ *Quiet and loud sounds*

Ask the children to close their eyes and listen to the sounds around them. Can they tell you which sounds are quiet and which ones are loud? The children can make a list of quiet sounds and a list of loud sounds. Does everybody agree that the sounds are quiet or loud? Ask the children to point to different quiet and loud sounds.

☐ *Sounds in the environment*

Repeat the above activities in various settings and ask the children to compare the different noises. Do sounds change from quiet to loud in different settings? Discuss why changes in our perception of loudness occur in different settings, such as a cough in the street compared with a cough in a library.

 Always be extremely cautious when carrying out activities where the child has her eyes closed or is blindfolded.

Environmental Sounds
ACTIVITIES FOR
Home

These activities will help your child to be more aware of sounds in her immediate environment. They also help to develop her skills in finding sound.

☐ **Early play**

Play peek-a-boo with your child. You can call your child's name. When she turns to look at you, call out "Boo!" Try hiding behind the curtains or sofa.

☐ **Sounds around**

Talk about the sounds your child can hear around her. Encourage her to find out who or what is making the sound.

☐ **Point to the sound walk**

Take your child for a walk. Stop and listen to the sounds around you. Ask her to point to the sounds you name. Can she do it with her eyes closed?

☐ **Hide-and-seek**

In the park or garden, hide from your child. Call her name and see if she can find you. (Warn her first before you disappear!)

 Always be extremely cautious when carrying out activities where the child has her eyes closed or is blindfolded.

Sounds &
SOUNDMAKERS

A variety of environments are suitable for finding sound games; for example:

- ☐ playground
- ☐ park
- ☐ shopping centre
- ☐ playing fields
- ☐ farm
- ☐ zoo

- ☐ wood
- ☐ nature park
- ☐ funfair
- ☐ street
- ☐ riverside
- ☐ seaside

Talk to your child's speech and language therapist/clinician or teacher about the places that interest you and your child. Ask them to tick appropriate places from the above list.

Finding Sound
CHECKLIST

Child's name	

Date	Activity	Comments
Example 3.7.	**Walk in the park**	**Turned to look at dog barking.**

Section 6: Finding Sound

FINE DISCRIMINATION

SECTION 7

INTRODUCTION

THE ACTIVITIES in this section help develop fine discrimination skills. They focus on two characteristics of sound, pitch and volume, which are demonstrated using musical instruments.

Children with a hearing loss often have difficulty in discriminating these characteristics. The activities can also be used to help concentration and memory skills in children with other communication difficulties.

Some children may be able to discriminate between sounds by the above characteristics without being able to identify the sound. For example, they may know when two drum beats have the same pitch level without knowing a drum made the sound.

Therefore the children are only required to decide whether two sounds are the same or different and to learn to respond to changes in pitch and volume. For older children, the concepts and vocabulary of pitch and volume can be introduced.

Listening to High and Low in Musical Instruments
TEACHING ACTIVITY

'Move this Way'

You will need:

a large floor area;
three wooden chime bars
(two identical low-pitched
bars and one with
a high pitch);
beaters; a screen.

Useful words
and phrases:

look, listen; chime bar;
skip; stride; wait; low;
high; same; different.

1 Introduce the low-pitched chime bars to the child. Demonstrate to the child how they look and sound the same. Let the child have a turn at playing with them.

2 Put these chime bars to one side when the child has finished playing and introduce the high-pitched chime bar. Let the child have a turn at playing with this one.

3 Next choose one low-pitched chime bar and make a sound, then beat the high-pitched chime bar. Talk about how the sound is different.

4 Explain to the child that you are going to play a listening game. Place one of the low-pitched chime bars in front of the child, but out of reach. Place the other bars behind the screen.

5 Make sure the child is ready and then tell her to listen carefully. Make a sound with the chime bar in front of child and then a second sound behind the screen, using either the low or the high-pitched bar. (Some children may need to hear the chime bar in front played two or three times *before* a sound is made by the bars behind the screen.)

6 Ask the child if the sounds are the same or different.

7 If she is incorrect, help her by letting her hear her chosen combination and then play the sounds again. So, if she incorrectly said, "Same", play two low notes and then a low and a high.

8 Once the child is consistently identifying when the chime bars have the same pitch, you can teach her to respond to the different pitches.

9 Explain to the child that you want her to stride across the room when she hears the sound of the low-pitched chime bar. Practise this activity until she is confident.

P

10 Next show her how to skip across the room when you play the high-pitched chime bar. Some children can be introduced to the terms 'high' and 'low'. Other children may need the bars identified by a colour or picture stuck on the side. A raised hand can be used to indicate a high-pitched sound and a lowered hand to indicate a low-pitched sound. Practise this activity until the child is confident.

11 Next make some sounds alternating between the two chime bars. Encourage the child to make the appropriate movements.

12 Hide the chime bars behind the screen. Can she do the activity by listening alone?

13 Stop her if she starts with the wrong movement and remind her which one she should be doing.

To increase the complexity of the activity:

◆ use fewer repetitions on the chime bar;
◆ make the difference in pitch between the two chime bars narrower;
◆ introduce a delay before the child is allowed to respond.

Variations

◆ Vary the movements the child has to carry out, such as hopping, walking slowly, doing bunny hops, walking backwards, walking sideways, crawling, walking with one foot behind the other, walking with a wide gait, stamping the feet, walking on tip-toe.

◆ Vary the musical instruments.

133

Listening to High and Low in Musical Instruments
ACTIVITIES FOR
School or Nursery

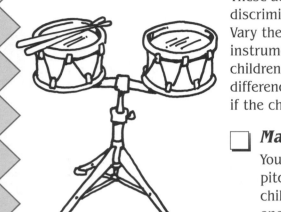

These activities help the children to practise their skills in discriminating high and low sounds in musical instruments. Vary the instruments you use but make sure you only use one instrument in each game: if the instruments are different, the children may be responding to the different sounds and not to a difference in pitch. Use hand gestures to indicate high and low if the children are unsure of the words.

☐ Match the drums

You will need two timpani drums which can be adjusted for pitch. Set the drums at different pitch levels. Ask two children to beat the drums as you slowly alter the pitch of one drum. The other children raise their hands when they hear the drums have the same pitch level.

☐ Action and movement games

You will need two chime bars. One bar should be low-pitched and one bar should be high-pitched. Play a low note and encourage the children to clap. Play a high note and encourage the children to stamp their feet. Hide the instruments and play different notes, alternating between the chime bars. Can the children match the action to different pitch levels?

☐ Team games

Divide the children into two teams. One team is told to listen for a high sound, the other to listen for a low sound. Demonstrate the two sounds on a piano or other musical instrument. The teams can only move across the room when they hear their note played. (The children could do small frog-jumps.) When the note changes they must stop and wait until they hear their sound again. The winning team is the first to cross the room.

☐ Solitaire

Let each child do the above game separately. The rest of the group watch and listen for a mistake.

Post it game

You will need two boxes and a musical instrument that has a high and a low-pitched note. Place one high up (for the high sound) and one low down (for the low sound). The children take it in turns to post an object in the appropriate box when they hear a sound from the instrument.

Christmas tree

Play this game with each child taking her turn to put a present on the tree. You will need one musical instrument that has a high and a low-pitched note. Draw a Christmas tree and several presents to be hung on the tree. When the child hears a high sound she can hang a present on the top of the tree. When she hears a low sound she can place a present under the tree.

Bridges

Either draw or make two bridges with several cardboard cut-outs of vehicles such as cars, buses, motorbikes and caravans. Place one bridge higher than the other. When the children hear a high sound from a musical instrument they must place a vehicle on the high bridge. When they hear a low sound from the same musical instrument they must place a vehicle on the low bridge.

Listening to High and Low in Musical Instruments
ACTIVITIES FOR
Home

These activities will help your child in listening for high and low sounds in musical instruments. Only use one instrument in each game, otherwise your child may be responding to the different instruments and not to a difference in the sound. Use hand gestures to indicate high and low if your child is unsure of the words.

☐ *Exploring high and low notes*

Use a recorder to show your child how to experiment with making high and low sounds. Let her make some sounds. When she plays a high note, stand on tip-toe and raise your hands above your head. When she plays a low note, crouch down on the floor. Stand with knees bent for notes in the middle. Play some notes for your child. Can she make the appropriate actions?

☐ *Magic Flute*

This is a super toy, available from Early Learning. This is like a flute, except that it has a sliding piece which can be moved up and down inside to vary the tone. Your child will enjoy experimenting with making the different sounds.

☐ *Hoop-la*

Play this version of 'hoop-la'. Your child must throw the ring onto a high peg when you play a high sound and onto a low peg for a low sound. Use two different chords on the same instrument to make the sounds. Start with two sounds that are very dissimilar. (If you do not have hoop-la, use tennis or pingpong balls with boxes placed at different heights.)

P

☐ *Hot and cold*

Hide an object from your child. To help her to find it, you can give her a clue using a musical instrument. Play a high note when she is close to the object. Play lower sounds if she moves away from the object. Xylophone, glockenspiel and piano are good instruments for this game.

☐ *Going up, going down*

Your child can pretend a musical instrument is a lift in a tall block of flats. Draw a picture and give the child a counter to move up and down as the lift. When the instrument makes a high note, the lift goes to the top floor. When the instrument plays a low note, it goes to the bottom floor. (Try this game using a rocket, the rising moon or a fireman climbing a ladder.) Xylophone, glockenspiel, piano or recorders are good instruments for this game.

Sounds &
SOUNDMAKERS

A variety of musical instruments or music makers can be used for listening to high and low sounds; for example:

- ☐ timpani drums (have adjustments to alter the pitch)
- ☐ tambour (has adjustments to alter the pitch)
- ☐ metal or wooden chime bars
- ☐ glockenspiel
- ☐ piano
- ☐ whistle or recorder
- ☐ bottles or porcelain bowls filled with different amounts of water (these produce differently pitched sounds when tapped with a metal spoon or knitting needle)
- ☐ guitar
- ☐ sonar resonator tone bars (these are particularly useful for the deaf and hard of hearing)
- ☐ xylophone
- ☐ Magic Flute

Talk to your child's speech and language therapist/clinician or teacher about the musical instruments that interest you and your child. Ask them to tick appropriate instruments from the above list.

Listening to Loud and Quiet in Musical Instruments
TEACHING ACTIVITY
'Making a Headband'

1 Introduce the drums to the child. Demonstrate to her how they look and sound the same. Let the child have a turn at making some sounds.

2 Tell the child that you are going to make a loud noise with the drum. Beat one of the drums several times. Help her to copy you in making a loud noise.

3 Then show the child how to make a loud sound using the other drum. Help her to copy you in making another loud sound. Talk about how the sounds are the same.

4 Tell the child that you are going to make a quiet noise with the drum. Beat one of the drums several times. Help her to copy you in making a quiet noise.

5 Next make a loud sound on one drum and a quiet sound on the other drum. Talk about how the sounds are different.

6 Explain to the child that you are going to play a listening game. Let her see you make the sounds at first, so that the strength of arm movement is a clue. Make a loud sound on one drum and either a loud or quiet sound on the other drum. (Some children may need to hear the loud sound played two or three times *before* a sound is made with the other drum.)

7 Ask the child if the sounds were the same or different. When she is consistent in responding, try hiding the drums behind a screen.

8 Continue the game with the child listening only.

9 If she is incorrect, help her by letting her hear her chosen combination and then play the target sounds again. So, if she incorrectly said, "Same", play two loud beats and then a loud and a quiet beat.

10 Once the child is consistently identifying when the drum beats are the same volume, you can teach her the following game.

11 Give the child some card and a felt-tip. Explain that when she hears a loud sound she must draw a big circle on the card, and when she hears a quiet sound she must draw a small circle. The card can be used to make a headband.

You will need:

two drums; a screen; beaters; narrow strips of stiff card that can be bent; coloured felt-tips; sticky tape.

Useful words and phrases:

listen; look; drum; quiet; loud; circle; small; big; wait; card; headband; felt-tip.

SECTION 7

139

To increase the complexity of the activity:

◆ use fewer repetitions on the drum;

◆ make the difference in volume between the drums narrower;

◆ introduce a delay before the child is allowed to respond.

Variations

◆ Make different patterns by using different shapes and colours: wide and narrow lines; small and large dots; small and large stars.

◆ The strips of card can be made into headbands, bracelets or necklaces by joining the ends with sticky tape. Other sizes and shapes of cards can be used to make badges, belts, book covers and pictures

◆ Vary the musical instruments.

Listening to Loud and Quiet in Musical Instruments
ACTIVITIES FOR
School or Nursery

These activities help the children to practise their skills in discriminating loud and quiet sounds in musical instruments. Vary the instruments you use but make sure you only use one instrument in each game. If the instruments are different, the children may be responding to the different sounds and not to a difference in volume. Use hand gestures to indicate loud and quiet if the children are unsure of the words. (Loud can be shown by wide outstretched arms and quiet by a pincer grip of the thumb and index finger.)

☐ *Movement to music*

Play loud and quiet music by turning the volume up and down on the radio. Get the children to move according to the volume of the music. A loud tune may have large steps and big arm movements. A quiet tune may have little skipping movements and gentle swaying.

☐ *Team games*

Use a drum for this game. Divide the children into two teams. One team is told to listen for a loud sound and the other to listen for a quiet sound. Demonstrate the two sounds on the drum. The teams can only move across the room when they hear their sound played. (The children could hop or skip.) When the sound changes, they must stop and wait until they hear their sound again. The winning team is the first to cross the room.

☐ *Solitaire*

Let each child do the above game separately. The rest of the group watch and listen for a mistake.

☐ *Pairs*

You will need four identical shakers or maracas. Four children are divided into two pairs. Each child in a pair is told to make a quiet or a loud sound, using the instruments. Make sure the children do not know who is making which sound. (Children could be given a symbol such as a large circle for a loud sound and a small circle for a quiet sound.) Each child in turn makes a sound. The two children who make the quiet sound must pair up and the two children who make the loud sound also pair up.

Put a counter on the loud sound

Play this game with individual children. Make a lotto card
with a big circle and a small circle marked on it. You will
also need several counters. Use a musical instrument to
make loud and quiet sounds. When the child hears a loud
sound she must place a counter on the big circle. When the
child hears a quiet sound she must place a counter on the
small circle.

Make a pattern

Ask the children to draw a big circle when they hear a loud
sound and a small circle when they hear a quiet sound. Use
a musical instrument to play alternating loud and quiet
sounds. The children can compare their patterns at the end.
Did everybody get the same pattern? Draw your own
pattern card for the children to make a comparison.

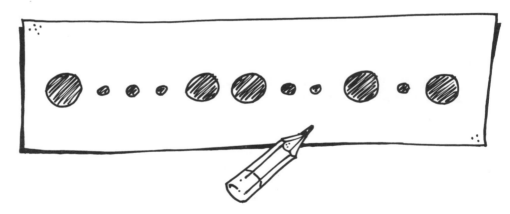

Listening to Loud and Quiet in Musical Instruments
ACTIVITIES FOR
Home

These activities will help your child in listening for loud and quiet sounds in musical instruments. Only use one instrument in each game, otherwise your child may be responding to the different instruments and not to a difference in the sound.

☐ ### Copy a loud sound

Experiment with making different sounds with a musical instrument. See if you can make some loud and quiet sounds. Help your child to copy the sounds you make. Talk about how some sounds are loud and some are quiet. Ask her which sounds she likes best.

☐ ### Movement to music

Play loud and quiet music by turning the volume up and down on the radio. Show your child how to make large steps and big arm movements to a loud tune and little skipping movements and gentle swaying to a quiet tune.

☐ ### Loud and quiet animals

Use a drum (a home-made one will do) to make loud and quiet sounds. When you make a loud sound, encourage your child to be a large animal, like an elephant. She can sway to the beat of the drum. When you play a quiet sound she can be a small animal, like a mouse. She can scurry about to the sound of the drum.

☐ ### Hot and cold

You will need a drum for this game. Hide an object in the room. Help your child to find it by beating a loud sound as she nears the object and quieter sounds if she moves away from it.

Sounds &
SOUNDMAKERS

A variety of musical instruments and music makers can be used in games using loud and quiet sounds. Remember that pitch can vary even in the same type of instrument and be an extra cue. Try to use one musical instrument for each game. Your choice might include some of the following:

- [ ] pali blocks and mallet
- [ ] wood blocks and mallet
- [ ] drum
- [ ] radio
- [ ] record player
- [ ] cassette player
- [ ] tambourine
- [ ] maracas
- [ ] shaker

Home-made musical instruments:

- [ ] empty biscuit tin and a wooden spoon (drum)
- [ ] frying pan or saucepan lid (gong)
- [ ] two sticks to tap together

Talk to your child's speech and language therapist/clinician or teacher about the musical instruments or music makers that interest you and your child. Ask them to tick appropriate instruments from the above list.

Fine Discrimination
CHECKLIST

Child's name	

Date	Activity	Comments
Example **30.5.**	**Movement to music**	*Enjoyed dancing to loud music. Not so keen on quiet.*

145

RHYTHM & SEQUENCING

SECTION 8

INTRODUCTION

THE ABILITY to copy a rhythm and recall the order of sounds presented in a sequence is an important aspect in the development of the child's auditory skills. Children with a hearing loss or specific language impairment often have difficulty in sequencing sounds and speech. The activities in this section will help the child to practise skills such as memory and ordering through the use of non-speech sounds. Many of the activities in other sections can also be modified to teach sequencing.

Identifying and imitating rhythms involves anticipation and recall. These skills will be utilized by the child when she later needs to sequence and order sounds into patterns. The following activities involve the senses of sight, hearing and touch. The child will learn to integrate what she sees, hears and feels and reproduce this through an action or movement.

Listening to the Number of Beats in Musical Instruments
TEACHING ACTIVITY
'Beat Out That Rhythm'

You will need:

two drums.

Useful words and phrases:

look; listen; drum(s); copy; beat; one; two; three.

1 This activity is best carried out with the child sitting next to you.

2 Explain to the child that you are going to play a listening game.

3 It is important to start with the child copying rhythms using her dominant side, whether this is right or left. Try to use the same hand as the child.

4 Let her watch as you beat out a pattern on one of the drums. Start with two beats (da-da).

5 Encourage the child to copy the beats using the other drum.

6 If she has difficulty, check that she can copy one beat and then, if necessary, physically manipulate her hands to beat out two beats. It may be necessary for you to use one drum and for you to beat out the rhythm together.

7 Once the child is confident in imitating two beats, you can introduce three beats (da-da-da).

8 Keep the beats evenly spaced and regular.

9 When the child is competent beating the rhythm alongside you, let her watch you and then try on her own.

To increase the complexity of the activity:

◆ increase the number of beats in the rhythm;
◆ ask the child to use her non-dominant hand;
◆ ask the child to listen with her eyes closed and then beat out the pattern;
◆ ask the child to use both hands: two hands on one drum or two drums;
◆ ask the child to alternate rhythms from one side to the other, for example right to left to right to left.

Variations

◆ Vary the musical instruments.
◆ Ask the child to carry out an action each time you beat the drum, for example to raise her arms.

Listening to the Number of Beats in Musical Instruments
ACTIVITIES FOR
School or Nursery

These games will help the children to develop simple rhythms. Keep the beats evenly spaced and of equal length. At first let them watch as you beat out the patterns; later they can try the activities with listening alone.

☐ Action to the beat

Beat out a single rhythm using a tambourine (for example, da–da–da). On each beat the children must carry out an action, such as raising their arms.

☐ Mark a pattern

Give the children some felt-tips and some paper. Ask them to make a mark each time you play a beat on the drum.

☐ Rhythm lotto

Play this game with a group of children or one child, using a xylophone or chime bars to make sounds. Draw a lotto card with nine squares. Mark in each square a dot to represent different numbers of beats on an instrument. So one dot indicates one note, two dots indicate two notes, several dots indicate several notes. The last line of the lotto card can be left blank for the child to complete. (See illustration.)

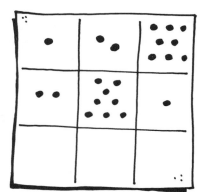

☐ Add up the numbers

You will need two drums with beaters to play this musical maths game for two. One child beats out a simple sum: for example, two beats – pause – two beats. The other child beats out the answer. In this case, four beats, of course! The children can watch each other at first, then try to do the sums by listening alone.

☐ Copy this beat

Use a drum to show the children how to play a simple two-beat rhythm, such as da–da. Ask each child to have a turn at copying it. Hide the drums behind a screen. Can the children copy the rhythm correctly when they are relying on listening alone? Let the children play rhythms for each other to copy. Can the children use both hands: two hands on one drum or a hand on each of two drums? Can they alternate rhythms from one side to the other, such as right to left to right to left?

Movement to the beat

Try these different movement games with the children.
You will need lots of space. They involve listening to the number of beats. Use a drum to beat out the rhythm:
one beat — the children must walk slowly until you say "Stop";
two beats — the children must walk quickly until you say "Stop".

Alternatively ask the children to shuffle across the room. When you play some beats on the drum they must stop and carry out the appropriate action:

one beat — jump one-quarter of a circle (so they are facing sideways);

SIDE   FRONT   '1 beat'

two beats — two quarter jumps (so they should be facing back where they came from);

FRONT   BEHIND   '2 beats'

three beats — three jumps that form three-quarters of a circle;

FRONT   BEHIND   SIDE   '3 beats'

four beats — four jumps that should bring the child in a full circle to face the front. Anybody facing the wrong way is 'out'.

SIDE   FRONT   BEHIND   SIDE   '4 beats'

Following a pattern

A group of children can play this game and get lots of listening practice. Draw a pattern of dots on a long strip of card. Choose one child to beat out the rhythm, for the other children to mark out the pattern. They can check their finished designs against the original pattern. Use several different designs so that each child in the group has a turn at beating out the rhythm.

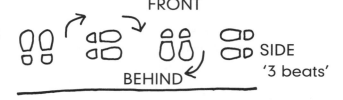

Listening to the Number of Beats in Musical Instruments
ACTIVITIES FOR
Home

These activities will help your child to copy simple rhythms using one hand. Let her watch as you beat out the rhythms. Hold her hand and beat out the rhythm with her.

☐ *Beat the drum*

You will need a drum and two beaters. Show your child a simple rhythm of two beats on the drum (da–da). Can she copy you, using her beater? Encourage her to play along with you. Increase the number of beats, but keep them evenly spaced (da–da–da). Can she copy the rhythm?

☐ *Clicking fingers*

Teach your child how to click her fingers. Can she copy a simple rhythm by clicking her fingers in time? Start with one hand and then see if she can click her fingers on both hands. Help her keep the clicks evenly spaced by getting her to slap her thigh in between each click. Can she click her fingers above her head, behind her knees and over her shoulder?

☐ *Tap out that rhythm*

Walk round the house and tap different objects. (Use a wooden spoon or knitting needle.) Ask your child to tap them with the same number of beats. Some may have two beats (da–da) others three (da–da–da). Encourage your child to keep the beats even. When your child is confident with this game, try tapping out a rhythm with both hands. You could use two sticks to tap out the beat on the same object, or tap twice on one object with one hand and twice on another with the other hand.

Sounds &
SOUNDMAKERS

Use different musical instruments to beat out rhythms; for example:

- ☐ tambourine
- ☐ tulip block
- ☐ wood block
- ☐ chime bars
- ☐ metal or wooden chime bars
- ☐ glockenspiel
- ☐ piano
- ☐ tabla
- ☐ bongo drums

Home-made musical instruments:

- ☐ empty biscuit tin and a wooden spoon (drum)
- ☐ two shells to tap together
- ☐ two sticks to tap together

Talk to your child's speech and language therapist/clinician or teacher about the musical instruments that interest you and your child. Ask them to tick appropriate instruments from the above list.

Listening to Long and Short in Musical Instruments
TEACHING ACTIVITY
'Colour My Chart'

1 Seat the child at a table.

2 Give her a piece of paper with rectangles drawn on it, as described right. Explain that you are going to play a listening game. You will be making some sounds. When she hears a long sound she must colour in one of the long rectangles. If she hears a short sound she must colour in one of the short rectangles.

3 Make a long sound and say to the child, "That was a long sound." Encourage her to colour in the long rectangle.

4 Make a short sound. Tell the child, "That was a short sound." Encourage her to colour in the short rectangle.

5 Next see if the child can colour in the rectangle without any help.

6 If she fails to make a response, repeat the sound. If she still has difficulty, tell the child whether the sound was long or short. Repeat it and help her colour in the appropriate rectangles.

To increase the complexity of the activity:

◆ reduce the difference between the long and short sound;
◆ use a quieter sound;
◆ increase the distance between you and the child;
◆ introduce a delay before the child is allowed to respond.

Variations

◆ Vary the sounds.
◆ Use different shapes or patterns.
◆ Use the coloured patterns for book covers or pictures.

You will need:

a recorder;
coloured felt-tips;
several pieces of paper.
Draw on a piece of paper
a long rectangle and next
to this a short rectangle.
(See illustration.)
Repeat this pattern
across the page.

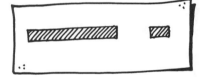

Useful words and phrases:

listen; look; wait;
felt-tips; long; short;
name of the musical
instrument.

SECTION 8

Listening to Long and Short in Musical Instruments
ACTIVITIES FOR
School or Nursery

These activities give the children experience of listening to long and short sounds in musical instruments. Let them watch first and then try the activities with listening alone. Use one sound for each activity.

☐ *Movement to long and short sounds*

Show the children how to make a movement when you make a sound on a musical instrument. This could be raising their arms above their heads. Explain to the children that you are going to make the sound longer. They must raise their arms and slowly lower them to the side until the sound stops. Alternate between long and short sounds so the children can see and feel the different movements. (Try using a recorder, flute or whistle.)

☐ *Long and short lotto games*

Two or three children can play this game. Make lotto cards that have six boxes. Draw either a long rectangle or a short rectangle in each of the boxes. Make each card different, so that some children have more long shapes and some more short. You will also need several counters. When the child hears a long sound she must place her counter on a long rectangle. When she hears a short sound she must place a counter on a short rectangle. Vary your presentation of the sounds: for example, two long sounds then a short sound. The winner is the first child to complete her card. (Try making sounds with a whistle, recorder or flute.)

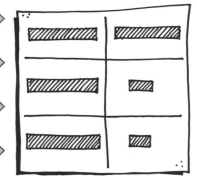

☐ *Making patterns*

Ask the children to draw a line when you play a note on a recorder. They must stop drawing when the sound stops. Make lots of long and short sounds. The children can compare their patterns at the end. Did everybody get the same pattern? Draw your own pattern card, for the children to make a comparison.

Listening to Long and Short in Musical Instruments
ACTIVITIES FOR
Home

These activities give your child experience of listening to long and short sounds using musical instruments. Some of the games encourage her to copy the sounds. Use one sound for each activity.

☐ *Recorder play*

Ask your child to draw a line when you play a note on a recorder. She must stop drawing when the sound stops. Make lots of long and short sounds. Your child can look at the patterns she has drawn at the end.

☐ *Blow the whistle*

Experiment with making sounds of different length by blowing into a whistle. Give your child another whistle so she can copy the sounds you make. Talk about how some sounds are long and some are short. Can she copy the sounds when you hide your face? (Do not worry if the sounds are not exactly the same length. Your child should be aiming just to make a difference between long and short.)

☐ *Station master*

Your child will have fun playing the station master in this game. You will need a toy train and a whistle. Explain to your child that the train can only move when the station master is blowing his whistle. Give your child the train and blow your whistle. Vary between short and long blows on the whistle, making sure your child stops the train when the whistle stops. Let her have a turn at making sounds for you to push the train. (Dress up in a cap and wave a red flag!)

Sounds &
SOUNDMAKERS

The following musical instruments can be used for long and short listening games:

- ☐ whistle
- ☐ recorder
- ☐ flute
- ☐ horn

Talk to your child's speech and language therapist/clinician or teacher about the musical instruments that interest you and your child. Ask them to tick appropriate instruments from the above list.

P

Listening to Fast and Slow in Musical Instruments
TEACHING ACTIVITY
'Parking the Car'

1 Introduce the drum to the child. Beat the drum quickly. Then beat the drum slowly. (Be careful to keep the volume the same when you change the rate of beating.)

2 Explain to the child that the cars need to be parked. Show her a parking space on the layout. When the drum is beaten quickly the cars can drive fast, but when the drum is beaten slowly the cars are crawling along in a traffic jam.

3 Place a car on a road on the layout. Let the child watch and listen to the drum before moving the car.

4 When she is consistent at responding appropriately to the drum, try a purely auditory activity. Place the drum out of sight behind a screen and repeat the activity. If the child is having difficulty, repeat the sound and, if necessary, let her see you make the sound.

5 Continue until all the cars have been parked.

To increase the complexity of the activity:
◆ use fewer repetitions of the sound;
◆ reduce the difference between a fast and slow beat;
◆ introduce a delay before the child is allowed to respond.

Variations
◆ Use different model vehicles, such as fire engines, police cars and ambulances.
◆ Instead of cars on roads, use trains on railway lines; aeroplanes taking off and landing at airports; animals moving into a field or Noah's Ark; miniature dolls running or walking slowly along the pavement.
◆ Let the child beat the drum.

You will need:

a floor layout of streets;
small model cars;
a drum with a beater;
a screen.

Useful words and phrases:

look; listen; fast; slow; car; parking; traffic jam; street or road.

S E C T I O N 8

Listening to Fast and Slow in Musical Instruments
ACTIVITIES FOR
School or Nursery

These activities help the children to practise their skills in discriminating fast and slow rhythms in musical instruments. Vary the instruments you use but make sure you only use one instrument in each game. If the instruments are different, the children may be responding to the different sounds and not a difference in pace.

☐ Dance to the beat

Listen to music with different beats. Encourage the children to move in time with the music. Help the children by beating out the rhythm on a drum.

☐ Change the rhythm

Use wood blocks to play this game. Create different patterns by using a combination of quick and slow beats. More able children can mark the beats onto a card. Each beat can be represented by a dot. A fast rhythm might have the dots closer together and vice versa for a slow rhythm. Write out a pattern on a card for the child to copy.

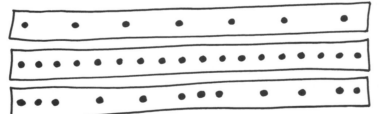

slow beat

fast beat

mixed beat

☐ Do the funky caterpillar

This game is great fun even if you do get a dirty bottom! Tell the children to sit on the floor in a long line with their legs outstretched. Each child should be sitting between the legs of the child behind. Explain that they are a caterpillar. They must grasp the ankle of the child behind with the left hand, and wave the right hand in the air. The children must shuffle along the floor like a caterpillar to the beat of a drum. When the rhythm changes from fast to slow or slow to fast the children must change direction. (The rocking movement and waving arms look most effective!) Two caterpillars can have a normal race or one line has to catch up with the other.

Listening to Fast and Slow in Musical Instruments
A C T I V I T I E S   F O R
Home

These activities will help your child in listening for fast and slow rhythms in musical instruments. Always use one instrument for each game so your child is listening to a change in pace and not a change in instrument.

☐ *Dancing*

Play music that has different beats for your child. Encourage her to dance quickly to fast music and slowly to music with a gentle beat. Quick steps could be skipping, hopping, side steps; slow steps could be knee bends, twirls on tip-toe and long strides.

☐ *Fast beat*

Experiment with making sounds at different speeds. Use a drum or a recorder. Play some quick beats, then some slow beats. Can your child copy the rhythm? (Do not worry if the rhythm is not exactly the same speed. Your child should be aiming just to make a difference between fast and slow.)

☐ *Hoisting up the sails*

Show your child how to 'hoist up the sails'. She should speed up for a fast beat and slow down for a slow beat. Beat out a rhythm for her on a drum or blow some notes on a whistle.

☐ *Pass the parcel*

Play this version of 'pass the parcel' at a party. The children pass a parcel around a circle in time to the beat of the music. When the rhythm of the music changes to a slow beat they must change direction and pass the parcel the other way. When the music stops, one wrapper of the parcel is opened. Continue with the game until all the layers are removed. The child who removes the last layer gets to keep the gift inside.

Sounds &
SOUNDMAKERS

A variety of musical instruments or music makers can be used for fast or slow rhythms; for example:

- ☐ drum
- ☐ triangle
- ☐ chime bars
- ☐ tambourine

- ☐ pali blocks and mallet
- ☐ hand-held bell
- ☐ guitar
- ☐ wood blocks and mallet

Home-made musical instruments:

- ☐ empty biscuit tin and a wooden spoon (drum)
- ☐ frying pan or saucepan lid (gong)
- ☐ two sticks to tap together
- ☐ plastic flower pot and a stick to tap together
- ☐ two saucepans lids to bang together

Talk to your child's speech and language therapist/clinician or teacher about the musical instruments that interest you and your child. Ask them to tick appropriate instruments from the above list.

P

Generalization of
RHYTHM SKILLS

Here are some suggestions for ways the child can generalize the skills she has learnt.

◆ Encourage the child to use her non-dominant hand.

◆ Show the child how to use both hands to beat out a rhythm.

◆ Give the child practice at recalling rhythms by listening alone.

◆ Show her how to use different parts of her body to beat out a rhythm, such as tapping her foot, clicking her fingers, clapping, stamping, drumming fingers, knocking.

◆ Try games that integrate a number of different rhythmic features. Examples include 'Pat-a-Cake' and other clapping games; skipping games; action songs, such as 'Wind the Bobbin up'; finger rhymes, such as 'Two Little Dicky Birds Sitting on a Wall'.

◆ Use musical instruments so that two hands are beating out the rhythm: for example, holding two maracas, banging two cymbals together or clicking castanets in each hand.

◆ Try dancing: Scottish, tap, square and flamenco all have a strong beat.

SECTION 8

Sequencing Musical Instruments
TEACHING ACTIVITY
'One, Two . . .'

You will need:

two identical pairs of musical instruments — two drums, two bells; a screen.

Useful words and phrases:

listen; look; wait; first; second; one; two; copy; drum; bells.

1 Check that the child is able to identify an instrument by sound alone.

2 Introduce the instruments to the child. Allow her some time to play with them and make some sounds.

3 Explain that you are going to play a listening game. Place one set of instruments in front of her within easy reach.

4 Seat yourself opposite the child with your matching instruments.

5 Tell her you are going to make two sounds. Ask her to watch and listen. Make a sound with one of your instruments. Explain that this is the first sound. Encourage her to copy you with her own instrument.

6 Make a sound with the other instrument. Explain that this is the second sound. Encourage her to copy you with her own instrument.

7 Repeat steps five and six but this time ask the child to wait until you have finished before she plays her instruments.

8 Encourage her to play the sounds in the same order as you.

9 Make sure that the child is confident at sequencing the two sounds by watching and listening, before trying a purely auditory task.

10 Hide your set of instruments behind a screen. Tell the child that you are going to make the first sound and then play that sound for several seconds. (Keep the child's attention focused on you so that she is ready to attend to the second sound.) Now tell her that you are going to make the second sound. Make the second sound for several seconds. Ask her to make the same two sounds as you.

11 If she has difficulty, repeat the sounds. If she continues to be unsure, ask her to copy the sounds one at a time. Then repeat both sounds for her to copy.

To increase the complexity of the activity:

◆ gradually increase the number of musical instruments (seven to eight maximum);

◆ increase the number of sounds to be sequenced;

◆ use musical instruments that sound increasingly similar;

◆ use fewer repetitions of the sound;

◆ use less familiar musical instruments;

◆ introduce a delay before the child is allowed to respond.

Variations

◆ Use different musical instruments.

◆ Ask the child to point to pictures of the instruments.

Sequencing Musical Instruments
ACTIVITIES FOR
School or Nursery

These games will help the child to learn about sequencing sounds from musical instruments. You will need to have duplicate sets of instruments for the children to copy the sequences.

☐ *Follow the leader*

You will need two or three pairs of matching musical instruments. Divide the pairs of instruments among a group of children. Two or three children each make a sound for the other children to copy in the same order. Can the children copy the sequence of sounds if the other children play their instruments out of sight?

☐ *Tape-recorder*

Record two or three sounds on a tape cassette. Can the children copy the sequence on the tape, using the real musical instruments?

☐ *Finish the sequence*

Get ready three musical instruments with matching pictures. Draw two large squares on a piece of card. Place one of the pictures on the first square. Place the other two pictures of musical instruments in view. Behind a screen, make the sound of the musical instrument in the picture on the first square. Play the sound of another instrument. The child has to complete the sequence by choosing one of the two pictures. Gradually increase the number of pictures the child has to sequence.

ACTIVITIES FOR
Home

These games will help your child to learn about sequencing sounds from musical instruments. You will need two sets of instruments: one set for you and one set for your child.

☐ *Pass the sound*

This game can be played with a group of children using simple musical instruments or by making the sounds themselves. One child makes a sound. The next child copies this sound and adds another. (It will be easier if the other children in the group can watch as well.) The game can be made harder by using sounds that are very similar, such as clicking fingers, tapping fingers in the palm.

☐ *Making music*

Use musical instruments or some home-made ones to create music. Show your child how to make two or three different sounds. Encourage her to copy the sounds you make. Can she make two or three sounds in sequence for you to copy?

Sounds &
SOUNDMAKERS

Try using a variety of musical instruments or music makers for sequencing games, such as the following:

☐ cymbals

☐ wood blocks and mallet

☐ jingle bells

☐ triangles

☐ castanets

☐ tone blocks

☐ tambourines

☐ glockenspiel

☐ pali blocks and mallet

☐ cabasa afuche

☐ tulip block

☐ Tibetan bells

☐ jingle stick

Home-made musical instruments:

☐ empty biscuit tin and a wooden spoon (drum)

☐ frying pan or saucepan lid (gong)

☐ two sticks to tap together

☐ silver foil bottle tops threaded on string

Talk to your child's speech and language therapist/clinician or teacher about the musical instruments that interest you and your child. Ask them to tick appropriate instruments from the above list.

1 Seat the child at a table. Make sure that she is able to identify the objects by their sound.

2 Show the child two of the empty jars.

3 Let the child see as you put a brick in one jar and some safety pins in the other. Replace the lids and shake each jar so the child hears the noise the object or objects make. Encourage the child to shake the containers.

4 Put the other brick and the rest of the safety pins in the remaining empty containers.

5 Explain that you are going to play a listening game. Place one set of jars in front of the child within easy reach. Seat yourself opposite her with your jars.

6 Tell her you are going to make two sounds. Ask her to watch and listen. Make a sound with one of your jars. Explain that this is the first sound. Encourage her to copy you with her matching jar.

7 Make a sound with the other jar. Explain that this is the second sound. Encourage her to copy you with her own matching jar.

8 Repeat steps five, six and seven, but this time ask the child to wait until you have finished before she shakes her jars.

9 Encourage her to make the sounds in the same order as you.

10 Wait until the child is confident at sequencing the two sounds by watching and listening, before trying a purely auditory task.

11 Hide your set of jars behind a screen. Tell the child that you are going to make the first sound and then make a sound for several seconds. (Keep the child's attention focused on you so that she is ready to attend to the second sound.) Now tell her that you are going to make the second sound. Make the second sound for several seconds. Ask her to make the same two sounds as you.

12 If the child has difficulty, repeat the sounds. If she continues to be unsure, ask her to copy the sounds one at a time. Then repeat both sounds for her to copy.

You will need:

two wooden bricks; several safety pins; four plastic see-through jars with removable lids.

Useful words and phrases:

look; listen; jar; brick; safety pins; shake; lid; one; two; first; second.

SECTION 8

169

To increase the complexity of the activity:

◆ gradually increase the number of object sounds (seven to eight maximum);
◆ shake the jar for a shorter period of time;
◆ increase the number of sounds to be sequenced;
◆ use objects that sound increasingly similar;
◆ use less familiar sounds;
◆ introduce a delay before the child is allowed to respond.

Variations

◆ Use different objects in the containers so that volume and pitch can be varied; for example, rice will sound different from marbles.
◆ Use different containers to alter volume or pitch. Marbles shaken in a tin will sound very different from those shaken in a plastic tub.

Sequencing Everyday Objects
ACTIVITIES FOR
School or Nursery

These games will help the child to learn about sequencing sounds. The materials are everyday objects. You will need to have duplicate sets of items for the children to copy the sequences.

☐ *Sequencing everyday sounds*

You will need two sets of everyday objects, such as two cups with two spoons, two wooden boxes filled with pencils. Place one set in view of the children. Use the other set to play a sequence of two sounds. Choose a child to copy the sequence using the duplicate set. Put the objects behind a screen. Can the children copy the sequence by listening alone? Gradually increase the number of object sounds to be sequenced.

☐ *Copy the sequence*

Play a group game. You will need two pairs of opaque jars and two different everyday objects, such as toy bricks and buttons. Place the objects in separate jars so that you have two matching sets. Give one set to two children. Choose another child to listen as the jars are shaken in turn, and then copy the order of the sounds with the matching set.

☐ *Follow the leader*

You will need three pairs of everyday objects. Distribute these among a group of six children. Choose three children to each make a sound. Can the other children copy the sequence of sounds using the matching everyday objects? Make the game harder by asking the children to make the sounds out of sight,

☐ *Regular routines*

A regular routine will provide the children with the experience of hearing a familiar sequence of sound.

SECTION 8

These games will help your child to learn about sequencing sounds. The activities use everyday objects to make the sounds. They also have ideas about everyday sequences.

☐ *Everyday sequences*

Draw your child's attention to the sequence of sounds in everyday activities. For example, washing has the sounds of running water, splashing, the plug being pulled in the basin. Other sequences are: making tea — kettle boiling, water being poured, spoon stirring in the cup, drinking; and having breakfast — cereal shaken from the packet, milk poured into the bowl, spooning up the food. Can you think of sequences of sounds that you hear every day?

☐ *Sounds on a walk*

Draw your child's attention to the sounds you hear on a walk to the shops or the nursery. Do you always hear the same sounds in the same order? Talk to your child about them. Show her how the order changes when you walk back or go a different way.

☐ *Copy a sequence*

You will need a couple of everyday objects. These could be buttons in a box or a spoon in a cup. Make sure you and your child both have one of the everyday objects. Show the child how you can make a sound with each object. Encourage her to copy you using her own objects. At first she may need to make sounds along with you. Later you can make the sounds out of sight. Can she copy the sequence by listening alone?

Sounds &
SOUNDMAKERS

A variety of everyday objects and small toys can be placed inside shakers or used in sequencing games. For example:

- [ ] spoon in a cup
- [ ] small toys or safety pins in a box
- [ ] keys
- [ ] coins
- [ ] beads in a box
- [ ] pegs or curtain hooks in a tin
- [ ] pebbles or stones
- [ ] cotton reels in a tin

(!) Always be extremely careful with small objects which may be swallowed accidentally by young children. Items should be placed in shakers with *secure* lids. If in any doubt, use larger objects or toys. Specialist children's stores, such as Mothercare, sell a device for checking whether objects are small enough to be swallowed.

Talk to your child's speech and language therapist/clinician or teacher about the soundmakers or sounds that interest you and your child. Ask them to tick appropriate soundmakers or sounds from the above list.

173

Rhythm and Sequencing
CHECKLIST

Child's name	

Date	Activity	Comments
Example **1.3.**	**Pass the sound**	**Copied three sounds but not in the right order.**

P

AUDITORY MEMORY

SECTION 9

INTRODUCTION

AUDITORY MEMORY is an important and integral part of listening and language skills. The child needs to process, store and retrieve information if she is to recognize and use sounds and speech in a meaningful way.

All listening activities involve memory to a certain extent, although different activities will have more or less of a memory load for the child. Advice is provided in this section on how to modify tasks to increase or decrease the memory load for the child in activities. Factors affecting the child's ability to remember auditory stimuli are also outlined.

FACTORS AFFECTING
the Child's Auditory Memory

The child's ability to remember auditory stimuli will be affected by the factors listed below, some of which relate to the child and others to the nature of the task presented to the child.

◆ *The child's hearing* — a child with a hearing loss will have difficulty with auditory memory. (Check whether the child wears hearing aids and, if so, that they are working.) Seek the advice of professionals such as a teacher of the deaf, audiologist, and specialist speech and language therapist/clinician (deafness).

◆ *The child's health and well-being* — a child who is tired, unwell or otherwise not comfortable will find it difficult to concentrate.

◆ *The child's language level* — a lack of language skills may make extra demands on the child's ability to complete an activity, thus affecting her memory capacity.

◆ *The child's familiarity with the adult* — the child may become withdrawn or 'play up' when with an unfamiliar adult.

◆ *Formal or informal situations* — it may be harder for the child to remember under the pressure of a situation where she is being tested. On the contrary, the child may be too relaxed in an informal atmosphere and be less inclined to concentrate.

◆ *Time pressures* — is there a time limit on the activity? Is it near dinner time? Is the child competing with another child? All these pressures may have an adverse effect on the child's ability to remember.

◆ *The age of the child* — memory skills are linked with language and develop with age.

◆ *The cognitive abilities of the child* — memory skills are linked with the cognitive level of the child.

◆ *A noisy background* — the child will be distracted and find it harder to listen with competing auditory stimuli.

◆ *A busy visual background* — the child will be distracted and find it hard to concentrate on two different types of stimuli: auditory and visual.

Memory loading can be increased by all of the following:

◆ new activities;
◆ unfamiliar materials;
◆ the amount of language the child is required to understand during the activity;
◆ a task involving several skills rather than one skill;
◆ auditory stimuli that are very similar;
◆ complex auditory stimuli;
◆ a delay before the child can respond;
◆ the level of listening skill: for example, sound detection is easier than sound recognition;
◆ the number of auditory stimuli the child has to choose between;
◆ the number of items the child has to remember;
◆ asking the child to recall a sequence;
◆ introducing a distraction before the child is allowed to recall items;
◆ the length of the activity.

When planning activities to develop memory, look at the suggestions for increasing the complexity of the activities in other sections of this manual.

ACTIVITIES FOR
School or Nursery

☐ **Sound diary**

First thing in the morning, ask the children to say what sounds they heard on the way to nursery or school.

☐ **What made that sound?**

Ask one child to close her eyes. Another child chooses an object or soundmaker and makes a noise. The child opens her eyes and finds the object to make the same noise.

☐ **Remember the soundmaker**

Introduce an unusual noise maker or musical instrument to the children each week. Can the children remember the object and the sound from the week before?

☐ **'Simon Says'**

Play 'Simon Says'. Gradually make the commands longer.

☐ **Name game**

How many names of children in the group can each child remember?

☐ **Beanbag**

Children throw a beanbag to each other. Before they throw the bag they must name the catcher.

☐ **Stories**

Tell the children stories based on pictures. At first let the children see the pictures, but later hide them so they have to listen to the speech. Can the children recall stories they have been told?

ACTIVITIES FOR
Home

☐ *Remember a rhyme*

Teach your child a simple rhyme. Can she remember to say it by herself?

☐ *Word games*

Play memory games where your child has to remember a list of words. Each person must repeat the phrase and the list of items and add a new one. If anyone forgets a word they are 'out'. Examples include:

I went shopping and bought . . .
I went to the zoo and saw . . .
I went on holiday and took . . .
I went to France and saw . . .

☐ *Nursery rhymes and action songs*

Learn a well-known rhyme or song with your child. Leave pauses for her to fill in the words or phrases. Start with the last word in a phrase and build up to a sentence: for example, 'Round and round the . . .'.

S E C T I O N 9

Auditory Memory
CHECKLIST

Child's name	

Date	Activity	Comments
Example 22.5.	*I went shopping*	*Likes this game. Remembered four items without help.*

LISTENING TO SPEECH

SECTION 10

INTRODUCTION

A CHILD develops spoken language through listening to speech and learning to imitate what she hears. Through a variety of experiences sound becomes meaningful to her and eventually she understands that a word represents an object, an event, a feeling or a person. Not only is she aware of speech, but she is also able to attach meaning to it. However, even at this stage of development, there are some children who find it difficult to listen to speech, even though they understand the words.

The activities in this section are designed to help those children who understand spoken language but who have difficulty in maintaining attention to speech. The games involve single words, simple commands and complex instructions. These are not activities for language teaching, although children's communication will be enhanced by any group activity involving interaction.

The activities are designed to develop listening skills and not comprehension of speech, so the vocabulary should be familiar to the child. You can check the child's understanding by asking her to name the items before you start the game. In general, children should start at the single-word level and build up to longer and more complex instructions. Remember that increasing the length and complexity of a command will increase the memory load for the child.

Single Words

The following games are based on the idea of 'information-carrying words' (see Knowles & Masidlover, *Derbyshire Language Scheme*). The number of information-carrying words in a sentence will affect the complexity of the utterance.

You will not be able to find the number of information-carrying words in a sentence by merely counting the words: the words give only part of the message. The child uses other information from the situation, such as gestural cues and what she has learnt from the past to help her to make sense of speech.

Some words in a sentence are redundant — they add nothing to the message. For example, the adult who says, "Give me the *ball*", while holding out her hand, is only requiring the child to understand 'ball'. The outstretched hand indicates to the child that the adult wants to be given something. This sentence, used in this context, will have one information-carrying word. If there is no other toy in the immediate vicinity of the child then 'ball' becomes redundant too. The child is likely to respond appropriately to the request even when she has not understood the verbal message.

Activities where the child is required to make a choice are likely to have information-carrying words. So if you ask the child for a banana, there must be the choice between the banana and another item. Otherwise it will be obvious to the child which object the adult is requesting. Key words for listening practice can be used alone or placed in a simple sentence where the other words are redundant. The following games require the child to understand one information-carrying word in the sentence.

Groups of Words for Listening Games with Single Words

- [ ] objects
- [ ] body parts
- [ ] prepositions
- [ ] animals
- [ ] food
- [ ] toys
- [ ] transport
- [ ] clothes
- [ ] occupations
- [ ] Action words, such as run, walk, sit, jump
- [ ] Girls' or boys' names
- [ ] Feelings, such as happy, sad, surprised

- [ ] Words with the same first sound

  sun, sea, sand: all have 's' at the beginnning

  boat, book, bat: all have 'b' at the beginning

  star, stair, stop: all have 'st' at the beginning

- [ ] Words with the same last sound

  cup, tap, map: all have 'p' at the end

  rat, bat, mat: all have 't' at the end

  first, last, mast: all have 'st' at the end

(If your child has a communication difficulty, consult a speech and language therapist/clinician on the suitability of these activities.)

Food
TEACHING ACTIVITY
'Let's Go Shopping'

You will need:

a shopping bag;
a variety of food items;
a table or other surface
that can be used as a
'pretend' shop counter.

**Useful words
and phrases:**

look; listen; food names;
go shopping; shop; bag.

1 Explain to the child that you are going to play a shopping game. Bring out each item of food for her to name.

2 Discard any she is unable to name, and place the remaining food on a table. The items should be spaced out so that each item is clearly visible.

3 Make it clear to the child that this is a 'pretend' shop.

4 Tell the child that you are going to play shops. Give her the bag and ask her to fetch an item from the shop: for example, "Can you buy me an apple?"

5 If the child is unsure, repeat the question or use a simpler request, such as "Apple". It may be necessary to point to the item or make a gesture, such as pretending to take a bite from an apple.

6 Ask the child to tell you what she has bought on her return with the bag.

7 Continue with the game until she has bought several items.

8 Can the child ask you to fetch some items?

To increase the complexity of the activity:

◆ gradually increase the number of items the child has to choose between (maximum eight to ten);
◆ increase the number of items the child has to remember;
◆ introduce a delay before the child is allowed to respond.

Variations

◆ Use empty food containers, such as cereal boxes, coffee jars or tins (do not use those that have a jagged edge from the tin opener) or try using plastic 'pretend' food.
◆ Play this game with a group of children. Make the children form a 'queue' or place mats on the floor as an imaginary path that each child has to follow. This will add a natural delay before the child is able to respond.
◆ Use certain groups of food. These might include vegetables; dairy products; meat; drinks; spreads; cereals; fish.
◆ Use food associated with special occasions such as festivals and religious events.

Food

ACTIVITIES FOR
School or Nursery

These games will help children with their listening skills. Although they will help communication skills, they are not designed specifically to teach language. It is expected that the children will know the vocabulary used in the listening activities.

☐ *Shopping trip*

Visit your local shops to show the children the different food for sale. Ask them to point to food as you name each item.

☐ *'Pretend' shop*

Set up a 'pretend' shop with either real food or 'pretend' items. You can play lots of games including some listening activities. Shopkeeper: one child is the shopkeeper and the other children are the customers. The children take turns to ask for an item of food. The shopkeeper finds the item and makes a sale. Shopper: the children line up to go shopping. Each child is asked to buy one item for you.

☐ *Restaurant*

Have a 'pretend' restaurant where one child is a waiter and the other children are the customers. The waiter must listen to the order from the children which she then tells to you — the chef. (Make a picture menu — see illustration.)

☐ *Puzzles and jigsaws*

Some puzzles and jigsaws have pictures of single food items. The child can be asked to take out and put back pieces that you name.

☐ *Doll play*

Ask the child for food items at a doll's tea party or during play in the home corner.

☐ *Post it*

Place on a table several large photographs of food. Ask the child to find pictures of different foods. They can post the correct one into a box.

ACTIVITIES FOR
Home

These are games to help your child listen to names of food. For listening activities it is important to use only food that your child knows and can name. Check her understanding of words by asking her to name the items of food before you use them in the games.

☐ *'Pretend' shops*

Use tins and other food items from the kitchen to play 'pretend' shops. Set up a shop on the table or floor. Give your child a plastic shopping bag and ask her to fetch one item at a time for you. For example, say, "Get me a banana." Let your child send you to the shops. She must tell you what items to buy.

☐ *Magazines*

Look through magazines with your child and talk about your favourite food. Ask her to find the pictures of different food: for example, "Where's the cake?" This could be her favourite food, something she had for dinner or an ingredient for a recipe. Help her cut pictures out to make scrapbooks or collages.

☐ *Find the . . .*

At the supermarket ask your child to find where the oranges are, then the bread, and so on. This will help her listening and stop her getting bored.

☐ *Shopping*

Ask your child to help you unpack the shopping. Ask for one item at a time.

☐ *Cooking*

Your child can help collect together the ingredients for a recipe or items for a meal.

Toys &
MATERIALS

Suggestions for toys and items that can be used to represent food are the following:

- [ ] real food
- [ ] 'Replica Food' — life-sized items, Winslow Press
- [ ] empty food containers
- [ ] *Plasticine* models
- [ ] papier-mâché models
- [ ] pictures from magazines and catalogues
- [ ] 'ColorLibrary (Food)' — photo cards, Speechmark Publishing
- [ ] 'Market Place' — photographs, LDA
- [ ] 'Photo Cue Cards (Food and Drink) – photographs, LDA
- [ ] line drawings

Talk to your child's speech and language therapist/clinician or teacher about the toys and materials that interest you and your child. Ask them to tick appropriate items from the above list.

Clothes
TEACHING ACTIVITY
'Teddy is off on Holiday'

You will need:

a teddy; a small toy suitcase; doll-size clothes.

Useful words and phrases:

look; listen; names of clothing; suitcase; teddy; holiday.

1 Explain to the child that teddy is going on holiday and that he needs some help with packing his suitcase.

2 Bring out each item of clothing for the child to name. Discard any she is unable to name, and place the remaining items on the floor.

3 Lay the clothes out so that each item is clearly visible.

4 Ask the child to fetch an item of clothing: for example, "Can you find teddy's jumper?"

5 If the child is unsure, repeat the question or use a simpler request, such as "Jumper". It may be necessary to point to the item or make a gesture, such as pretending to pull a jumper over your head.

6 Ask the child to tell you what she has found before she packs it away in teddy's suitcase.

To increase the complexity of the activity:

◆ gradually increase the number of items the child has to choose between (maximum eight to ten);

◆ increase the number of items the child has to remember;

◆ introduce a delay before the child is allowed to respond.

Variations

◆ Use real articles of clothing.

◆ Instead of a suitcase, try a duffle bag; shoulder bag; cardboard box; shoe box; briefcase (a colourful plastic one); string bag; sports bag; child's suitcase; pillow case; basket.

◆ Vary teddy's holiday destination: warm climate versus cold climate; beach holiday versus country holiday.

◆ Introduce other holiday items, such as sunglasses, sun cream, bucket and spade.

Clothes

ACTIVITIES FOR
School or Nursery

These games will help children with their listening skills.
Although they will help communication skills they are not
designed specifically to teach language. It is expected that the
children will know the vocabulary used in the listening
activities.

☐ *'Pretend' shop*

Set up a 'pretend' clothes shop using old clothes, baby or
doll's clothes. Lay several items out on a table or other
surface that can be used as a counter. You can play lots of
games including some listening activities. Shopkeeper: one
child is the shopkeeper and the other children are the
customers. The children take turns to ask for an item of
clothing. The shopkeeper finds the item and makes a sale.
Shopper: the children line up to go shopping. Each child is
asked to buy one item for you.

☐ *Play 'Simon Says'*

Play a dressing-up game using a version of 'Simon Says'.
Have lots of items of clothing, such as hats, gloves, shoes,
scarves and waistcoats. The children must put on the
clothes only when you say, "Simon says...", otherwise they
are out of the game.

☐ *Team competition*

Divide the children into two teams. One child is chosen
from each team to be the 'clothes horse'. Make sure there
is a very large pile of clothes, such as hats, gloves, shoes,
scarves and waistcoats for the children to sort through. The
other children must dress their team member in the items
of clothing you call out. The first team to finish dressing is
the winner.

☐ *Doll play*

Play dressing-up games with a doll and some doll's clothes.
Ask the child to dress the doll in the items as you name
them.

S E C T I O N

10

Musical clothes

This is a version of musical chairs, but in this game the children must find an item of clothing to wear. You will need lots of clothes with several sets of the same item, such as hats or scarves. Before the start of the game, sort the clothes so that for the first turn of the game there should be enough items for all the children. For the second turn there should be one less than is needed, and so on until there is only one item of a particular piece of clothing: for example, five hats, four scarves, three pairs of gloves, two belts and one jacket. The children move around while you play some music. When the music stops you call out an item of clothing, such as "Hat". The children must find a hat and put it on. The child who fails to find an item of clothing is out. Continue with the game and choose a different item of clothing next time. The last child 'in' is the winner.

Post it

Place several large photographs of clothes on a table. Ask the child to find pictures of different clothes. They can post the correct one into a box.

Matching pictures to clothing

You will need several photographs or pictures of clothing with real items to match. Name different articles of clothing for the child to find and match to pictures or photographs. Choose clothes that are part of a theme: for example, sports clothes, school clothes, winter clothes, uniforms, clothes associated with different countries, cultures or festivals.

Washing line

Hang a washing line up in the room. Use real clothes, doll's clothes or cut-outs. Ask the children to hang up the clothes you name. Instructions could also be given by a puppet or doll: "Hang up my coat."

Clothes
ACTIVITIES FOR
Home

These games will help your child with her listening skills. For listening activities it is important only to use clothes your child knows and can name. Check her understanding of words by asking her to name the items used in the games.

☐ *Fashion show*

Play at being a catwalk model with your child! Ask her to find different items of clothing for you to model. You can then do the same for her.

☐ *Magazines and clothes catalogues*

Look through magazines or clothes catalogues with your child. Ask her to find pictures of different items of clothing. This could be her favourite party dress or swim-suit. If you are ordering clothes, maybe she could help you find the picture and reference number. Or help her cut pictures out to make scrapbooks or collages.

☐ *Doll play*

Play dressing-up games with a doll and some doll's clothes. Ask your child to dress the doll in the items as you name them. You can use a real doll or put paper clothes on a cardboard cut-out figure.

☐ *Dressing*

When your child is dressing, ask her to fetch different clothes to put on. Avoid asking for the items in the order of dressing, otherwise she can guess what you want!

☐ *Laundry*

Ask your child to sort your laundry, saying, for example, "Find all the blouses." Can she put away your ironing as you name the items?

Toys &
MATERIALS

Try using the following items in listening games with a clothes theme:

- [ ] real clothing
- [ ] doll's clothing
- [ ] baby clothes
- [ ] pictures from magazines and catalogues
- [ ] 'Photo Association Cards (Clothes)' — photographs, LDA
- [ ] 'Photo Cue Cards (Clothes)' — photographs, LDA
- [ ] line drawings
- [ ] cardboard cut-outs
- [ ] paper dolls and cut-out clothes

Talk to your child's speech and language therapist/clinician or teacher about the toys and materials that interest you and your child. Ask them to tick appropriate items from the above list.

Body Parts
TEACHING ACTIVITY
'Give Dolly a Bath'

1 The child may need to wear an apron and roll her sleeves up, as this game involves water play.

2 Introduce the doll, washing items and bath to the child and explain that dolly needs a bath.

3 Show the child how to lather up the sponge with the soap. Talk to the child as you wash different parts of the doll: for example, "Now I'm washing dolly's hands."

4 Let the child have a turn. Hand her the sponge and ask her to listen carefully. Tell her, "Wash dolly's hands."

5 If the child is unsure, repeat the instruction or use a simpler command, such as "Wash hands." It may be necessary to point to the doll's hands or make a gesture, such as showing her your hands.

6 Continue the activity, naming different parts of the body.

To increase the complexity of the activity:
◆ gradually increase the number of body parts to wash: for example, "Wash dolly's *hands* and *feet*";
◆ introduce a delay before the child is allowed to respond.

Variations
◆ Use a teddy instead of a dolly.
◆ When you have finished bathing dolly, encourage the child to use the towel to dry parts of dolly as you name them: for example, "Dry dolly's back."

You will need:

a large doll;
a plastic baby bath
filled with tepid water;
a sponge; a bar of soap;
a towel; an apron.

Useful words and phrases:

look; listen;
names of body parts;
wash; dry; bath; water;
soap; sponge; towel.

S E C T I O N 10

Section 10: Listening to Speech

Body Parts

ACTIVITIES FOR
School or Nursery

These games will help children with their listening skills. Although they will help communication skills they are not designed specifically to teach language. It is expected that the children will know the vocabulary used in the listening activities.

☐ *Point to your . . .*

Ask the child to point to body parts on herself or other children. Children can have fun by sticking gold stars on different body parts.

☐ *Find the picture*

Place several pictures or photographs of body parts on the table or floor. Ask the child, "Where is the picture of a hand?" and so on. Make the game more fun by turning the pictures face down.

☐ *Picture lotto*

Ask the child to find pictures of body parts that you name and then match them to a picture lotto.

☐ *Draw an outline*

Using large sheets of paper, ask the child to draw round different parts of her own body and parts of other children's bodies.

☐ *Draw a body part*

Draw a giant outline of a body. The children can take turns in drawing parts of the body that you can name.

☐ *Nursery rhymes and action songs*

Nursery rhymes and action songs provide the children with repetitive phrases and words. Try stopping before the last word, for the children to join in. Some are useful for teaching words on a particular theme, such as "This is the way we wash our face; this is the way we comb our hair' (body parts and action words) or 'Shoulders, heads, knees and toes' (body parts).

198

Early Listening Skills

Body Parts
ACTIVITIES FOR
Home

These games will help your child with her listening skills. For listening activities it is important only to use body parts your child knows and can name. Check her understanding of words by playing the copying game (see below) first.

☐ *Copying game*

Point to your eyes as you name them. Encourage your child to copy you.

☐ *Show me . . .*

Ask your child to show you different body parts as you name them: for example, "Show me your eyes."

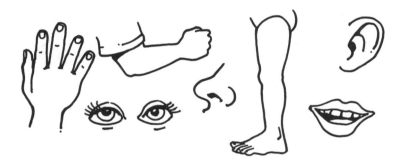

☐ *Bath time*

Ask your child to wash different body parts at bath time. (Change the order around each day.) Have a game with your child to see if she can guess which part is next. Dolly or teddy can have a bath too. Tell your child, "Wash dolly's hair" or "Wash dolly's face."

☐ *Nursery rhymes and action songs*

Nursery rhymes and action songs provide your child with repetitive phrases and words. Try stopping before the last word for your child to join in. Some are useful for teaching words on a particular theme, such as 'This is the way we wash our face; this is the way we comb our hair' (body parts and action words) or 'Shoulders, heads, knees and toes' (body parts).

☐ *Picture books*

Look at people in picture books. Can your child point to the different body parts as you name them?

S
E
C
T
I
O
N

10

Toys & MATERIALS

Try using the following items in games using the names of body parts:

- [ ] pictures from magazines or catalogues
- [ ] 'Head, Hands and Feet' — photographs, LDA
- [ ] 'Body Parts' — photographs, LDA
- [ ] line drawings
- [ ] *Plasticine* models of body parts
- [ ] papier-mâché models of body parts
- [ ] body parts on teddies and puppets
- [ ] body prints: for example, paint your hand and make a print
- [ ] shadows cast by body parts
- [ ] front, back and side views of body parts

Talk to your child's speech and language therapist/clinician or teacher about the toys and materials that interest you and your child. Ask them to tick appropriate items from the above list.

Animals
TEACHING ACTIVITY
'Farmyard Animals'

1 Show the model farm to the child.

2 Bring out each animal piece for the child to name. Discard any she is unable to name and replace it with another animal she is able to name. Place the animals outside the farm. Make sure each piece is clearly visible to the child.

3 Explain to the child that all the farmer's animals have escaped: "Can you help the farmer to find the lost animals and bring them safely home?"

4 Ask the child to find an animal: for example, "Where's the cow?"

5 If the child is unsure, repeat the question or use a simpler request, such as "Cow". It may be necessary to point to the item. When the child has correctly selected the animal, she can place it in the farmyard.

6 Continue until all the animals are in the farmyard.

You will need:

three small plastic animal shapes (for example, a cow, a pig and a horse); a model farm.

Useful words and phrases:

look; listen; animal names; farm/farmyard; farmer; escape; lost.

To increase the complexity of the activity:
◆ gradually increase the number of animals the child has to choose between (maximum eight to ten);
◆ ask the child to find more than one animal at a time;
◆ introduce a delay before the child is allowed to respond.

Variations
◆ Vary the animals.
◆ Use a zoo and appropriate animals rather than a farm.
◆ Hide the animals around the room.

S E C T I O N 10

201

Animals

ACTIVITIES FOR
School or Nursery

These games will help children with their listening skills. Although they will help communication skills they are not designed specifically to teach language. It is expected that the children will know the vocabulary used in the listening activities. These games will help with listening to animal names.

☐ *Noah's ark*

Make a large cardboard cut-out of Noah's ark. Draw different animals on the side of the ark. Have matching animal pictures. Ask each child to find the picture of the animal you name and place it with the other animal in the ark. Use *Blu-tack* or similar to secure the pictures.

☐ *Animal race*

Have a race! Give the children different miniature animals that have to jump several hurdles. (Use plastic toy fences from a farm set or make your own with empty match boxes.) Each animal can only jump a hurdle when its name has been called.

☐ *Picture lotto*

Draw or stick animal pictures on a lotto board. Have matching flashcards. Take one card but do not allow the child to see the picture. Name the animal. The child must point to the animal on the lotto board. If the child is correct she can have the card to place on the board. (A group of children can play this game and have a competition to see who finishes first.)

☐ *Draw an animal*

Place several plastic animal shapes in the middle of the table. Name an animal for each child to draw.

☐ *Animal farm*

Ask the children to help you set up a model farm. Use a toy farm and animals. Name the animals you want the children to place on the farm.

☐ *Matching animal shapes to pictures*

You will need several miniature animal pieces with matching animal pictures. Ask the child to find an animal and place it on the matching picture.

Animals
ACTIVITIES FOR
Home

These are games to help your child listen to animal names. For listening activities it is important only to use animals your child knows and can name. Check her understanding of words by asking her to name the animals before you use them in the games.

☐ Animal noises

Name an animal. Can she make the appropriate noise, such as 'moo' for a cow, 'neigh' for a horse?

☐ Animal masks

Make large, colourful animal masks. The child puts on the appropriate mask when you name the animal. Encourage her to mime the animal's movements and copy the sounds it makes.

☐ Visit a farm or zoo

Ask the child to find different animals as you walk round the farm or zoo. There are many 'city farms' where your child will enjoy stroking and feeding the animals. When you return home, draw a picture of an animal you saw on your visit. Ask your child to draw an animal for you.

☐ Story books

Look at animal pictures in a book. Ask your child to find different animals as you name them. You can make the animal sounds together.

☐ Animal posters

Find posters or large pictures that portray several different animals, for example a jungle scene, or animals at a zoo. Ask your child to point to the animals as you name them.

☐ Puzzles

Many early puzzles have animals as a theme. Ask your child to take out and put back the animals you name.

S
E
C
T
I
O
N
10

Toys & MATERIALS

Toys and materials that can be used to represent animals include the following:

☐ cuddly toys

☐ 'Animal Sounds' — photographs, Taskmaster

☐ 'Photo Sound Lotto (Animals)' — LDA

☐ 'Look Hear (Animals)' — LDA

☐ *Outdoor Sounds ColorCards* — Speechmark

☐ *Animals & Birds ColorLibrary* — Speechmark

☐ pictures from magazines

☐ line drawings

☐ *Plasticine* models

☐ papier-mâché models

☐ animal puppets

☐ animal masks

☐ cardboard cut-outs

Talk to your child's speech and language therapist/clinician or teacher about the toys and materials that interest you and your child. Ask them to tick appropriate items from the above list.

Action Words
TEACHING ACTIVITY
'Make Dolly Dance'

1 Introduce the doll to the child. Show her how to move her arms and legs to make her dance, sit, jump, lie down, walk and run.

2 Let the child have a turn at copying these actions with the doll.

3 Ask her to make the doll carry out an action: for example, "Make dolly dance."

4 If the child is unsure, repeat the question or use a simpler request, such as "dance". It may be necessary to move your body in imitation of dancing or to show the child the action with the doll.

5 Continue with the game until the child has tried several actions.

To increase the complexity of the activity:
◆ ask the child to perform more than one action with the doll: for example, "Make dolly *jump* and *sit down*";
◆ introduce a delay before the child is allowed to respond.

Variations
◆ Use a teddy instead of a doll.
◆ Ask the child to name actions for you to carry out with the doll.

You will need:

a doll with movable legs and arms.

Useful words and phrases:

look; listen; doll; dance; walk; run; sit down; lie down; jump.

SECTION 10

ACTIVITIES FOR
School or Nursery

These are games to help children with their listening skills. Although they will help communication skills they are not designed specifically to teach language. It is expected that the children will know the vocabulary used in the listening activities. These games will help with listening to action words.

☐ *Playground games*

Ask the children to carry out different actions. Try jumping, hopping, skipping.

☐ *Pictures*

Gather together several pictures of people carrying out various actions. Hide these around the room. Ask the children to find different pictures: for example, "Where is the picture of someone jumping?"

☐ *Actions*

Use miniature animal figures which have different positions, such as lying down, sitting, standing or eating. Ask the children to find different animals: "Show me the one eating", and so on. (Only have one animal for each action.)

☐ *Obstacle course*

Set up an obstacle course for the children. Let them take it in turns to go round the course. Ask each child to carry out different actions as they come to an obstacle. For example, a mat can be jumped over, walked round or hopped across.

Action Words

ACTIVITIES FOR
Home

These are games to help your child with her listening skills. For listening activities it is important only to use action words your child understands and can name. Check her understanding of words by asking her to name the actions used in the games.

☐ **'Simon Says'**

Play 'Simon Says'. Give your child an action to carry out, such as "Jump".

☐ **Make dolly jump**

You will need a doll or teddy with movable arms and legs to play this game. Show your child how to make different actions with the doll. Ask your child to make the doll carry out different actions: for example, "Make dolly jump."

☐ **Ball games**

Ask your child to carry out different actions with a ball. These could include throwing, rolling, kicking and catching.

☐ **Action songs**

Sing action songs with your child. Leave pauses for her to do the actions named in the song.

S
E
C
T
I
O
N

10

Toys & MATERIALS

Try using the following items in listening games using action words:

- [ ] pictures from magazines of people carrying out actions
- [ ] teddy or other toy with movable limbs
- [ ] plastic animals with movable limbs
- [ ] puppets
- [ ] real people!
- [ ] dolls made from pipe-cleaners

Talk to your child's speech and language therapist/clinician or teacher about the toys and materials that interest you and your child. Ask them to tick appropriate items from the above list.

Listening to Single Words
CHECKLIST

Child's name	

Example 2.12.	Shopping game	Food	Fetches items when asked. Says name.

Simple Commands

The complexity of a command or instruction will be determined by one or more of the following: (1) number of information-carrying words, (2) length of sentence, and (3) concepts.

Sentences that involve two information-carrying words have at least two key words within the sentence that the child must understand before she can carry out the command or instruction appropriately. Activities will involve the child in making a choice for each of these key words. For example, the command, "Give me the *red book*" may involve the use of a red book, a blue book, a red pencil and a blue pencil. The child must choose between the book and the pencil, and the colours red and blue. (Note that if you hold out your hand, she does not have to understand the word 'give'.)

Some simple commands can make use of the child's everyday knowledge of events. The command, "Put the *doll* on the *chair*" only has two information-carrying words. The word 'on' is redundant as it is usual for people to sit *on* a chair. Therefore the child does not need to understand this word. Once a different preposition is introduced, as in "Put the *doll under* the *chair*", the child has to understand three words and the command becomes more complex.

The length of the sentence can be increased by asking the child to fetch two items, as with "Bring me dolly and teddy, please." Other sentences could include "Show me"; "Give me"; "Put the"; "Find the" and "Where are". Names can also be used to increase length, as with "Find Farouk and Jessie, please."

A simple command may include one or more of the following concepts (remember this will also increase the memory load):

◆ size (big, large, small, little)
◆ length (long, short)
◆ weight (heavy, light)
◆ position (under, on, in, next to, behind, near to)
◆ action words (jump, run, hop, skip, clap)
◆ colour (red, yellow, blue, orange)
◆ number (one, two, three, many, few, lots)
◆ texture (smooth, shiny, rough, scratchy)
◆ taste (sweet, sour, salty)

Prepositions
TEACHING ACTIVITY
'The Obstacle Race'

1 Set out the equipment so that it forms a natural obstacle course with a clear path to follow.

2 Tell the children that they are going to have an obstacle race. They must listen very carefully as they will be told which way they must go round the obstacle course. If they make a mistake they must start again.

3 Explain that each child will be timed and the winner will be the one who has the fastest time.

4 Select the first child and give her an instruction. Start with simple instructions and build up to longer and more complex commands: for example, "Go *under* the *table*"; "*Run to* the *hoop*"; "*Crawl* through the tunnel *backwards*" or "*Go round* the *chair*". Only give one instruction at a time.

5 Keep instructions fairly simple and within the child's language competence. If the child has difficulty, repeat the instructions or use a gesture, such as pointing underneath with your hand.

6 Continue the activity until all the children have completed the course.

7 Select the child with the shortest time as the winner.

To increase the complexity of the activity:

◆ introduce more than one command;
◆ gradually increase the length of the instructions;
◆ gradually increase the complexity of instructions by including different prepositions and action words;
◆ introduce a delay before the child is allowed to respond.

Variations

◆ Split the group into two teams. Each team member is given a different set of instructions to follow. The winning team is the one with the fastest time. It may be best to set up two courses when using two teams!
◆ Ask the children to go round the obstacle course in a certain sequence, for example, Mary, Carlos, Fatima.
◆ After you give the instructions, make the children wait for a starting bell, whistle or flag.

You will need:

a large floor space; large physical play equipment, such as play tunnel, hoops.

Useful words and phrases:

look; listen; obstacle race; obstacle course; names of equipment; action words; on; under; through; in; behind; in front of; over.

S E C T I O N 10

ACTIVITIES FOR
School or Nursery

These are games to help children with their listening skills. Although they will help communication skills they are not designed specifically to teach language. It is expected that the children will know the vocabulary used in the listening activities. These games will help with listening to simple commands using prepositions.

☐ *Team races around an obstacle course*

Set up an obstacle course. Divide the children into two teams. Each team member receives instructions from you on which way to go round the course. Introduce the concepts of size and colour by using big and small boxes or different coloured hoops. Commands could include "*Jump* into the *blue* hoop." The team with the quicker time is the winner.

☐ *Sports and games*

Give the child instructions to follow in the gym or during games. Commands could include "Jump over the mat" or "Climb along the wall bars."

☐ *Instructions*

Give the child instructions to follow in the nursery room. These could include "Stand behind your chair" or "Get in line under the clock".

Prepositions

ACTIVITIES FOR
Home

These are games to help your child with her listening skills. For listening activities it is important only to use prepositions your child understands. These games will help with listening to simple commands using prepositions.

☐ ### 'Simon Says'

Play 'Simon Says'. Give your child different actions to carry out, using prepositions such as under, on, behind or in: for example, "Lie under the table" or "Sit behind the sofa."

☐ ### Hide dolly

You will need a small doll or other suitable figure with movable arms and legs to play this game. Tell your child where to hide the doll. Dolly could hide under the carpet or in the sewing box. Can your child tell you where to hide dolly?

☐ ### Put away the shopping

Ask your child to help you put away the shopping. Use requests such as "Put the sugar behind the biscuit tin" or "Put the washing-up liquid under the sink."

☐ ### Tidying up

During the day ask your child to tidy up. Use commands that involve prepositions, such as "Put your satchel under the bed" or "Put your football behind the chair."

SECTION 10

Equipment &
MATERIALS

You may carry out similar games with a variety of equipment such as the following:

- ☐ large physical play equipment
- ☐ furniture, such as chairs, tables and rugs
- ☐ areas marked out on the floor with chalk or string
- ☐ naturally occurring obstacles outside, such as trees, boulders
- ☐ very large sheets of paper
- ☐ sturdy boxes
- ☐ hoops
- ☐ large building bricks

Talk to your child's speech and language therapist/clinician or teacher about the equipment and materials that interest you and your child. Ask them to tick appropriate items from the above list.

Please remember to use equipment that is safe, and do not ask your child to carry out any physical actions that might endanger her. Make sure there are no hard surfaces in case she should fall while climbing. Be aware of your child's physical needs and capabilities, and seek the advice of a physiotherapist if your child has physical disabilities.

Animals
TEACHING ACTIVITY
'Animals in their Place'

1 Introduce the farmyard set to the child and check that she knows the names of the different parts of the farm, such as pond and shed.

2 Bring out each animal for her to name. Discard any she is unable to name and replace it with another animal she is able to name. Place the animals on the floor. Make sure each piece is clearly visible.

3 Explain to the child that all the farmer's animals have escaped and are wandering around in the wrong parts of the farm: "Can you help the farmer put the lost animals into the right places on the farm?"

4 Ask her to place one of the three animals in a part of the farm: for example, "Put the *cow* in the *field*."

5 If the child is unsure, repeat the command.

6 If the child picks up the cow but is unsure where to place it, help her by pointing to the field.

7 If the child points to the field but does not attempt to pick up the cow, help her by pointing to the cow.

8 Continue the game, asking the child to follow various instructions.

To increase the complexity of the activity:

◆ ask the child to place the animal in an unexpected place, for example a cow in the pond;
◆ gradually increase the number of animals (maximum eight to ten);
◆ gradually increase the length of the command by asking for more than one animal; for example, "Put the cow and the pig in the shed";
◆ gradually increase the complexity of the command by including colour and action words in the command; for example, "Put the brown horse in the shed" or "Put the cow that is lying down in the field";
◆ introduce a delay before the child is allowed to respond.

Variations

◆ Use different animals.
◆ Use a farm layout rather than a model.
◆ Other animal themes could include a zoo; pets' corner; working animals (farm, police); sea-life (sea, sand, rock pool); insects (earth, flowers, stones — use pictures!).

You will need:

three small plastic animal shapes (for example, a cow, a pig and a horse); a farmyard model with fields, a pond and sheds for the animals; a small plastic figure of a farmer.

Useful words and phrases:

look; listen; animal names; farm; farmer; escape; pond; field; shed.

SECTION 10

215

Animals

ACTIVITIES FOR
School or Nursery

These are games to help children with their listening skills. Although they will help communication skills they are not designed specifically to teach language. It is expected that the children will know the vocabulary used in the listening activities.

☐ *Stick up a picture*

You will need a large picture of a farm and several pictures of farm animals. Name two or three animals the child must stick on the picture. (Use *Blu-tack* or a similar material to make the pictures stick.)

☐ *Draw an animal*

Place several plastic animal shapes in the middle of the table. Name two or three animals. When the child has found the shapes, she can draw round them.

☐ *Animal farm*

Ask the children to help you set up a model farm. Use a toy farm and animals. Name the animals you want the children to place on the farm: for example, "Put the cow, the pig and the horse on the farm." Include colour or action words in the commands, such as "Show me where the brown horse is" or "Give me the cow lying down." Many plastic animals come in different colours and in different attitudes. (Use other themes, such as animals at the zoo or animals at the circus.)

Animals

ACTIVITIES FOR
Home

These are games to help your child listen to simple commands involving the use of animal names. For listening activities it is important only to use animals that your child knows and can name. Check her understanding of words by asking her to name the animals before you use them in the games.

☐ Story books

Look at animal pictures in a book. Ask your child to find two animals. Can she remember both names? Try with three animals.

☐ Animal posters

Find posters or large pictures that portray several different animals: a jungle scene, a picture of animals at the zoo, and so on. Ask your child to point to two animals as you name them. Can she remember both?

☐ Hide the picture

This game is for two children. You will need several pictures of animals. One child leaves the room while you tell the other child where to hide the pictures. Give the child the picture before you give the command. Use commands like "Put the tiger under the table." When the other child comes back, ask her to find two or three animals.

☐ Make a giant picture

Make a giant picture of the seaside, a farm or the garden. Have lots of places where animals might live. The garden could have a rockery, a tree, flowers and a bush. Help your child draw some animals, or cut pictures from magazines. Ask her to stick the animals in different places: "Put the bird in the tree" and so on. Once she has got the idea, you can introduce some unusual requests, such as "Put the cat in the tree" and "Put the bee in the rockery."

SECTION 10

Toys & MATERIALS

Toys and other items that can be used to represent animals include the following:

- [ ] photographs
- [ ] pictures from magazines
- [ ] line drawings
- [ ] *Plasticine* models
- [ ] papier-mâché models
- [ ] animal puppets

Instead of a model farm, try the following:

- [ ] a farm layout mat
- [ ] sheds made out of boxes
- [ ] ponds made out of silver foil
- [ ] a large composite picture of a farm

Talk to your child's speech and language therapist/clinician or teacher about the toys and materials that interest you and your child. Ask them to tick appropriate items from the above list.

Furniture
TEACHING ACTIVITY
'Moving House'

1 Introduce the doll's house to the child and check that she knows the names of the different rooms.

2 Bring out each piece of furniture for her to name. Discard any she is unable to name, and place the remaining pieces in the toy van. Make sure each piece is clearly visible to her.

3 Tell the child that she is going to pretend to be a removal person. She must help deliver the furniture to the house and make sure each piece of furniture goes in the right room.

4 Ask her to place a piece of furniture in a room in the house: for example, "Put the chair in the living room."

5 If the child is unsure, repeat the command.

6 If the child picks up the chair but is unsure where to place it, help her by pointing to the room.

7 If the child points to the living room but does not attempt to pick up the chair, help her by pointing to the chair.

8 Continue the game, asking the child to follow various instructions.

To increase the complexity of the activity:

◆ ask the child to place the furniture in an unexpected place, for example the bath in a bedroom;
◆ gradually increase the number of pieces of furniture (maximum eight to ten);
◆ gradually increase the length of the command by asking for more than one piece of furniture;
◆ gradually increase the complexity of the command by including size and position words in the command; for example, "Put the small chair in the bathroom" or "Put the sofa next to the fireplace";
◆ introduce a delay before the child is allowed to respond.

Variations

◆ Stick pictures of furniture on a layout of a house.
◆ Other themes for using furniture names include a school (classroom, office, hall); a hospital (waiting room, doctor's office, ward); a shopping centre (toy shop, chemists, book shop).

You will need:

*toy furniture;
a small doll's house;
a large toy van which allows miniature furniture to be placed inside.*

Useful words and phrases:

*look; listen; house;
removal/removal van;
names of furniture;
names of rooms in a house.*

SECTION 10

Furniture
ACTIVITIES FOR
School or Nursery

These are games to help children with their listening skills. Although they will help communication skills they are not designed specifically to teach language. It is expected that the children will know the vocabulary used in the listening activities.

☐ *Rearrange the room*

Use simple commands to get the children to rearrange the room: for example, "Put the table in front of the window."

☐ *Doll's house*

Use toy furniture and a doll's house for this game. The children tell each other how to arrange the furniture.

☐ *Small dolls*

Use miniature figures and doll's house furniture. Commands can include the following: sit on; lie on; push; pull; stand next to; stand behind.

☐ *Furniture shop*

Set up a 'pretend' furniture shop using toy pieces of varying sizes and colour. The children can take it in turns to shop for a 'new house'. They can ask for 'a red chair' or 'a big table' and so on.

☐ *Obstacle course*

Use real furniture to set up an obstacle course. Give the children commands that involve the furniture, such as "Walk to the table."

ACTIVITIES FOR
Home

These are games to help your child listen to simple commands involving the use of names of furniture. For listening activities it is important only to use furniture that your child knows and can name. Check her understanding of words by asking her to name the pieces of furniture before you use them in the games.

☐ *Hiding games*

Play this game with several children (maybe at a party). One child is the seeker and should leave the room while the other children hide. Give the children instructions on where to hide, using names of furniture; for example, "Hide behind the sofa."

☐ *Catalogues*

Ask your child to find two pieces of furniture in a catalogue or magazine; for example, "Find a chair and a table." Can she remember both pieces of furniture? She can cut out the pictures and make a collage.

☐ *Doll's house*

You will need toy furniture and a doll's house for this game. Tell your child where to place the items of furniture; for example, "Put the table in the kitchen." Pretend to be removal people. (You could wrap the furniture in newspaper or put the items in boxes!)

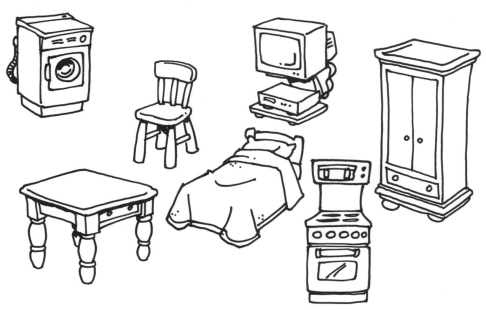

Toys & MATERIALS

Try using the following items to represent furniture:

- ☐ photographs
- ☐ *Home ColorLibrary* — Speechmark
- ☐ pictures from magazines and catalogues
- ☐ line drawings
- ☐ *Plasticine* models
- ☐ papier-mâché models

Talk to your child's speech and language therapist/clinician or teacher about the toys and materials that interest you and your child. Ask them to tick appropriate materials from the above list.

Listening to Simple Commands
CHECKLIST

Child's name	

Date	Activity	Commands	Comments
Example **31.1.**	Doll's house	"Put the table in the bedroom"	Enjoyed putting pieces inside doll's house. Mixed up cupboard and wardrobe.

S E C T I O N

10

Complex Commands

A complex command or instruction will have one or more of the following constituents: (1) multiple information-carrying words, (2) increased length of sentence, (3) complexity, and (4) a number of concepts.

The child is required to understand at least three information-carrying words within the sentence before she can carry out the command or instruction appropriately. The activity will need to be structured so that the child has to make a choice for each of the key words. For example, the command, "Put the *doll under* the *bed*" may involve the use of a doll, a teddy, a bed and a table. The child must choose between the doll and the teddy, and between the table and the bed. The preposition 'under' is also an information-carrying word as the doll could also go in, on top of, behind or next to the bed. Remember to contrast prepositions and use unusual positions; otherwise the child can use her everyday knowledge of events to guess that the doll goes 'in' the bed.

The length of the sentence can be increased by asking the child to fetch several items, as with "Bring me an apple, an orange, a pear and a banana, please." Other sentences could include "Show me"; "Give me"; "Put the"; "Find the" and "Where are". Names can also be used to increase the length, as in "Touch Paul, Peter, Mita and Kay, please."

The type of grammatical constructions used in the sentence will affect complexity. A sentence with a subject, verb, object (SVO) construction is a simple format that can easily be developed into a complex command. "The cow is in the field" can be used as the basis of "Put the black cow in the field." Compare the complex grammatical instruction, "Put the book, lying on the red table, in the tray" with the simpler type of command, "Put the book in the tray."

A complex command may include one or more of the following concepts (remember this will also increase the memory load):

◆ size (big, large, small, little)
◆ length (long, short)
◆ weight (heavy, light)
◆ position (under, on, in, next to, behind, near to)
◆ action words (jump, run, hop, skip, clap)
◆ colour (red, yellow, blue, orange)

◆ number (one, two, three, many, few, lots)

◆ texture (smooth, shiny, rough, scratchy)

◆ taste (sweet, sour, salty)

The activities used earlier in this section can be modified to include more complex instructions.

Examples of Activities

◆ *Shopping game*

Ask the child to fetch a big apple
    or two bananas
    or the heaviest potato
and put it in a bag
    or a basket
    or a box

For example, "Fetch me a big apple and put it in the basket." (There should be a choice between a basket and another type of bag. Similarly there should be a big and a small apple amongst the food items.)

◆ *Teddy's going on holiday*

Ask the child to find teddy's blue T-shirt
    or big jumper
    or shiny scarf
and put it in his bag
    or suitcase
    or duffle bag
    or box

For example, "Find teddy's big jumper and put it in his duffle bag." (There should be a choice between a duffle bag and another type of bag. Similarly there should be a big and a small jumper amongst the clothes items.)

◆ *Give dolly a bath*

Ask the child to comb dolly's hair
    or wash teddy's hands and feet
(Include a teddy with the dolly.)

◆ *Obstacle race*

Ask the child to carry out actions and then move to a named place. For example, "Touch your *nose* and walk to the *window*." The complexity can be increased as you include more choices: "*Rub* your *nose* and walk to the *window*"; "*Rub* your *nose* and *run* to the *window*"; or even "*Rub Halil's nose* and *run* to the *door.*" (In this activity the child has a choice of body part, action on the body part, place, and action to get to the place.)

Listening to Complex Commands
CHECKLIST

© Diana Williams 1995

Child's name	

Date	Activity	Comments
Example 4.5.	**Simon Says**	**Able to carry out three actions.**

P

LISTENING SKILLS IN THE SCHOOL CURRICULUM

SECTION

11

INTRODUCTION

THE ACTIVITIES in this section are based on the requirements of the school curriculum in terms of speaking and listening skills. They are aimed at older children who are able to take part in discussions. They provide opportunities for the children to work co-operatively as partners, in small groups or as a whole class. The use of a variety of communication styles is encouraged.

Examples are given of ways in which listening and sound can contribute to the children's learning and enjoyment of subjects such as maths, English and science.

The topic work provides the child with the opportunity to listen, understand and express ideas in a variety of contexts and in a variety of modes. It encourages children to explore and discover sounds and the sense of hearing.

The School Curriculum

Listening skills are vital for the young child if she is to participate in the learning experiences presented to her in school, whether in the use of listening as a learning medium, or in sound and hearing as an area of study.

Listening and speaking in themselves are key elements within the school curriculum. In all areas of study the child will be expected to listen to spoken descriptions, questions, instructions and explanations, not only from her teacher but from fellow pupils. During discussions she will have to learn to listen to the views and ideas of others.

Maths

Traditional methods of teaching in maths have relied on rote learning in the form of chants or recitation (for example, simple counting, times tables and number rhymes) and this continues to be a useful way of memorizing figures. The subject of maths also requires the child to make comparisons, order, sort and identify patterns. The use of discussions by small groups of children is helpful for this type of problem solving. Children can listen to each other, first to clarify their understanding of the task, and then to make predictions and share solutions.

Science

Part of the curriculum in science involves developing an understanding of the way our body works and in particular the five human senses. Children enjoy learning about the senses of touch, taste, smell, sight and, of course, hearing as they are able to experience what they are being taught. The ear, and how we hear, can be linked with discovering what sound is, how sound travels and how it can be measured.

In science children need to listen to and answer questions such as why? where? when? and how? These questions form the basis of their observations and investigations. They will need to recall events in order to describe and explain results.

English

Rhymes, songs, poems and stories read aloud all require the child to listen. They also provide repeated sound and word patterns that form the first steps on the pathway to literacy. Sounds and noises can be used to help the child appreciate the written word by enlivening the text, as with sight and sound books. Children can listen to stories on the radio and television, or hear a classmate retell a familiar tale.

Discussion by the class of written material such as poems and books will help the development of spoken language. Children can be encouraged to develop and respond to different opinions. Talking in groups about favourite stories and characters will also enhance the child's understanding and enjoyment of books.

Topics

HThe following topics can be used to help develop the children's speaking and listening skills as well as supporting the curriculum in key subject areas.

What is Sound?

Children can:

◆ find out about sound and how it is transmitted;

◆ make a list with a partner of the different sounds that occur at home, at school or at the youth club;

◆ discuss the uses of sound — to communicate by spoken language, as a warning (a fire alarm, for instance), to enjoy, as in music;

◆ discover how sound is measured;

◆ experiment with making different sounds and then discuss the similarities and differences between two sounds;

◆ listen to sounds and synthesized speech made by computers;

◆ try out experiments with a string telephone, echo chamber or recording studio.

Why is Hearing Important?

Children can:

◆ find out about the ear and how we hear;

◆ listen to sound through different mediums, such as headphones or an ear trumpet;

◆ experience being deafened by putting ear plugs in the ears to block out sound and to describe what it feels like not being able to hear (ear plugs are available at most large chemists or drug stores).

If you are helping children to experience being 'deaf' make sure you supervise them well. They should always be escorted if they go outside the classroom. Make sure the area is safe and that you have removed any dangerous obstacles for this activity.

- discuss issues about deafness – difficulties faced, advantages (such as not being disturbed by noise at night!), aids for deafness;
- learn sign language (have a finger spelling competition, where the children have to learn to spell a certain number of words);
- explain why they think hearing is important to them;
- experiment with ways of communicating messages without the use of speech (including facial expression, body language and gestures as well as writing and pictures);
- discuss noise pollution, drawing up a set of guidelines for their school;
- find out how to take care of their hearing, for example avoiding excessive noise, and not poking objects in the ear.

Musical Instruments

Children can:

- compare the sound made by different groups of musical instruments, such as wind instruments with string instruments;
- discuss the different methods of making sound used by musical instruments;
- make their own instrument;
- listen to instruments from different countries, grouping together similar instruments, such as guitar, banjo and ukulele;
- discover the history of musical instruments and describe how they have changed through the ages;
- do a project on an orchestra, steel band or pop-group (the children could visit a performance and the project could be presented to the school as part of an assembly);
- gather information about musical instruments used at different festivals and religious ceremonies, find out why these particular instruments are used and describe the mood and atmosphere these instruments create;
- make a tape recording of all the different sounds the class can make using their voices, tongues and lips;
- use musical instruments to 'paint a sound picture' of a busy high street or a nature trail;
- learn to make sound effects and create sounds to accompany a piece of film or a television advertisement.

Music and Singing

Children can:

◆ learn and perform a well-known folk song for the school assembly;

◆ compare the acoustics of singing in the playground with singing in a hall;

◆ carry out a survey among the other children in the school to find out the top ten pop stars — the results can be written in a table;

◆ attend a music performance;

◆ create a simple dance or set of movements with a partner to fit a piece of music, each pair performing in front of the other children;

◆ bring their favourite album, cassette or CD and explain to the class why they like it so much;

◆ choose a piece of music and find pictures, colours, shapes and objects they feel are associated with that style of music: for example, a rock and roll piece might have bright pinks and yellows with roller skates, hair cream and a photo of Elvis! The children can explain why they have chosen certain items;

◆ ask their parents what music and songs they liked when they were the same age;

◆ do a project on the songs and music of a particular era, looking at the historical background and how this affected the music, for example songs in the Second World War and the Great Depression;

◆ compare two interpretations of a pop song (the children may be surprised to hear an older version of a 'new' pop song);

◆ bring in recordings of music that is important or well known in their culture;

◆ make up their own music, using poems or stories to stimulate ideas;

◆ visit a theatre and hear how music is used in drama.

Media

Children can:

◆ discuss the term 'media';

◆ listen to a programme on the radio or television and report back to the class;

◆ visit a television or radio station;

◆ discover the history of the media;

◆ write their own newspaper, each child taking it in turn to read a piece aloud;

◆ debate why sound is important in the media;

◆ make their own films on video or record a radio play, experimenting with making sound effects;

◆ write a review of their favourite television programme;

◆ discover how sound was introduced into the movies;

◆ make a silent movie and discuss the differences in acting style between silent films and 'talkies'.

Environment

Children can:

◆ talk about the sounds they hear at school and compare these with the sounds they hear at home or in their local street;

◆ carry out a survey of the sounds that people like and hate — the results can be put into the top ten best loved sounds and the top ten most hated sounds;

◆ discuss the sounds they most love and hate, explaining what makes them feel that way;

◆ talk about noise pollution in the city and in the countryside and find out what help is available to curb noise nuisances;

◆ look at how and why noise has changed in the environment through history;

◆ compare the sounds in the environment made by man and the sounds made by nature;

◆ look at the way sounds in the environment change with the seasons;

◆ compare sounds that might be heard in different countries;

◆ measure the sounds they hear;

◆ have a sponsored 'silence'.

Communication

Children can:

- 'brainstorm' what communication means;
- experiment with communicating one message using different means, including verbal and non-verbal methods;
- compare methods of communication that involve spoken language with methods that use other means, for example a telephone versus a fax;
- list the advantages and disadvantages of different methods of communication;
- talk about the different languages in the world and how they came about;
- learn the same word (for example, "Hello") in different languages — children who speak other languages can help;
- learn how the deaf and the deaf—blind communicate;
- discover how communication has changed through history and what inventions have brought about these changes;
- think what life would be like without one of the modern forms of communication, such as the telephone, and discuss what they would miss and why.

HOLIDAY PROJECTS

SECTION

12

INTRODUCTION

THIS SECTION has numerous suggestions for reinforcing the child's listening skills and expanding her auditory experiences. Activities range from special visits to places of interest to more everyday experiences such as attending a playgroup. These activities are aimed at parents who may want to continue working on their child's listening skills during school holidays or a break from therapy. Some ideas may be new to parents, while others may reassure them that the activities their child participates in already will enhance her listening. There should be an activity to suit all parents, regardless of financial or social needs. Some are for whole family participation and others are for the child alone. The parents are encouraged to keep a record of activities and how their child responds to sounds.

Holiday Listening Projects

Below are some ideas for helping your child's listening skills during the holidays. They include places to visit, special events and ideas of how you can join in the fun. Check your local paper for dates of special activities or details of places to visit. There is often lots of information at your local library about coming events. Look out for free entry or special rates for children.

☐ ### Special days
Many local councils, community centres, hospitals, schools and day nurseries organize or take part in special event days for users of their services. Activities range from fun days to sports competitions. Whatever the theme, it is guaranteed to stimulate the senses, including the ears and eyes.

☐ ### Puppet shows
Children love puppet shows and Punch and Judy still provide popular entertainment at the seaside. The stories are fun and the children enjoy listening to the different voices while watching the action!

☐ ### Clowns
Although clowns have no speech, there are lots of bangs, whooshes and honks to interest your child.

☐ ### Music festivals
These can be enjoyed by all the family and they may even have a children's music workshop.

☐ ### Religious festivals
When your children attend a special religious ceremony or festival they are learning about the sounds and music that are important in expressing their religious beliefs. It is also important for the child to experience times of quiet.

☐ ### Dance exhibitions
These can be organized events that your child may wish to take part in or a spontaneous expression by street entertainers. Remember that music must accompany the dancing, so your child is listening as well as watching.

P

Parades or carnivals

Watch the colourful procession and listen to the music! You may want to join in with the dancing or singing. Your child can march along beside a big brass band. Or she can skip, dance and clap to the strong beat of Afro-Caribbean music.

Funfairs

Children of all ages love funfairs. There are many sights, sounds and smells to excite your child before she even takes her first ride. Many sounds are associated with the ride itself — the music of the carousel and the thump as the bumper cars crash. Look out for mini funfairs at the seaside, often found on the end of the pier.

Holidays

If you are on holiday or visiting your family in another country, your child will experience many new and different sounds. But you do not have to go abroad to give your child new experiences. A change of scene will also provide different noises and voices. A different town, a new house or even a different routine can stimulate your child's interest in the sounds around her.

Special exhibitions at museums

During holidays many museums hold special exhibitions that are of particular interest to children. The 'living museum' is a popular way of portraying life in the past. This way the child can hear, feel, smell and see the past. So dinosaurs come to life with a roar, a horse shoe is hammered out in a Victorian smithy and music plays on an old gramophone.

Some museums have an emphasis on sound and listening. The Museum of the Moving Image in London specializes in radio, television and film history. There are numerous exhibitions that encourage active participation by the child, including an opportunity to read the news, take part in a television interview and star in a Hollywood film. Find out about your local museums.

Historical sound and light shows

These types of show are becoming more and more popular. They consist of reconstructions of scenes from the past, using lifelike models with special effects from sound and light. Some famous ones include Canterbury Tales at Canterbury and the vikings at York. As these can be expensive, you might like to save this for a treat.

☐ Children's theatre

Do you have any local workshops or drama groups for children? Taking part in a children's theatre will involve your child in exploring and experimenting with her voice.

☐ Play groups, play centres and crèches

Here your child will meet other children and have the opportunity to take part in a variety of activities that are not feasible at home, such as hand and foot painting! These organizations may also provide outings for your child that will expand her listening experience.

☐ Story time at the library

Many libraries have a special time during the day when stories are read aloud for children. This helps the child with listening and concentration, as well as introducing her to story books.

Write down your own ideas about holiday activities you can do with your child.

Holiday Projects
CHECKLIST

Child's name	

Date	Activity	Comments
Example **4.4.**	***Playgroup***	***Likes playing with the musical instruments.***

SECTION 12

LISTENING RESOURCES

SECTION

13

INTRODUCTION

A LISTENING box contains all the materials which you may use for listening activities. This section has suggestions for various soundmakers that can be collected and kept in this box.

A listening resource for either adult-directed activities or independent learning is a listening tape. Rhymes, songs, music and stories can be recorded on audio tape. Associated toys and games can be collected. For example, the song 'Old MacDonald's Farm' might be accompanied by a book of animal pictures or miniature figures. A number of suggestions for making different tapes are given in this section.

Listening Box

Make your own listening resource box. The following objects can be collected and kept together in a large box.

- ☐ bell
- ☐ assorted pairs of musical instruments
- ☐ squeaky toys
- ☐ shakers
- ☐ everyday objects for shakers (see p259)
- ☐ scrunchy paper
- ☐ musical and noisy mobiles
- ☐ electronic key finder
- ☐ alarm clock
- ☐ metronome
- ☐ buzzers
- ☐ hooters
- ☐ music box
- ☐ musical cards
- ☐ musical and noisy toys
- ☐ sea-shells
- ☐ books with sound makers, such as buzzers

Listening Tape

Make a tape of rhymes, songs and stories. Collect related objects and pictures for the child to play with while listening to the tape. She can listen alone or do the activities with an adult who can prompt her if necessary. (These suggestions are based on an idea in *Play Helps*, by Roma Lear.)

Songs

◆ 'Old MacDonald's Farm' — give the child a set of miniature animals to hold while she makes the animal sound in the song.

◆ 'The Wheels on the Bus' — use a large floor puzzle of a bus for the child to piece together. During the song the child can point to the wheels, the passengers on the bus, and so on.

◆ 'Ring-a-Ring-of-Roses' — the child can dance to the music.

Rhymes

◆ 'Two Little Dicky Birds Sitting on a Wall' — have two finger puppets for the child to wear as she sings the song.

◆ 'Humpty Dumpty Sat on a Wall' — a soft toy in the shape of Humpty Dumpty can be bought from toy shops. He can fall off a table, the back of a chair or a real wall.

Stories

◆ 'The Gingerbread Man' — write a recipe card for gingerbread men. The biscuits baked by the child can be used to act out the story and then be eaten!

◆ 'Little Red Riding Hood' — the child acts out the story using puppets, a bed and a forest scene painted on cardboard.

◆ 'Three Billy Goats Gruff' — the child acts out the story with three different sized toy goats and a troll. A bridge can be made out of stiff cardboard.

◆ 'Three Little Pigs' — the child acts out the story with toy pigs. The child can help make the different houses or paint them on card. The wolf can be a puppet. The child will enjoy blowing down the houses.

Music

Picture books, tapes and videos are often produced to accompany popular children's films. The child can look at the pictures of her favourite film as she listens to the theme music. She may like to join in with the songs and dance along to the rhythm.

Theme Tapes

You may want to use a tape that follows a particular theme or topic. A tape with animals as the theme may have the following activities:

- [ ] 'Three Blind Mice', with a recipe card to make sugar mice;
- [ ] 'Old MacDonald's Farm', with animal puppets to wear;
- [ ] 'Jungle Book' theme music with matching pictures;
- [ ] animal sounds to copy and animal face masks to wear.

EVERYDAY SOUNDS & SOUNDMAKERS

SECTION

14

INTRODUCTION

THIS SECTION provides a comprehensive list of sounds, noises, words and soundmakers for use in listening activities. These suggestions can be used by parents, carers and teachers to stimulate ideas for adapting and extending activities and games. Using a variety of sounds and soundmakers will help the child to generalize her listening skills. It can also be used to indicate appropriate sounds and soundmakers for a specific child.

Musical Instruments

'Musical Instruments Box':

a large, sturdy storage box, filled with a wide range of musical instruments ranging from jingle taps to glockenspiels and hand drums. There are pairs of each instrument. Available from Winslow Press (see Appendix II: Resources).

The following musical instruments can be obtained from good quality music shops:

- [ ] jingle bells
- [ ] glockenspiel
- [ ] headless tambourine
- [ ] wood blocks and mallet
- [ ] castanets
- [ ] tone blocks
- [ ] pali blocks and mallet
- [ ] cymbals
- [ ] bells
- [ ] shekere
- [ ] bongo drums
- [ ] tabla
- [ ] cabasa afuche
- [ ] wooden agogo
- [ ] round bell xylophone

- [ ] tulip block
- [ ] Tibetan bells
- [ ] jingle stick
- [ ] shaker stick
- [ ] tambour
- [ ] slit drums
- [ ] triangles
- [ ] hand bells
- [ ] guitar
- [ ] drum
- [ ] tone bars
- [ ] sonar resonator tone bars
- [ ] mouth organ
- [ ] recorder

Home-made instruments:

- [ ] drum — empty biscuit tin and a wooden spoon

- [ ] gong — frying pan or saucepan lid suspended by cord

- [ ] percussion instrument — tap two wooden sticks together; tap a flower pot with a stick

- [ ] shaker — silver milk bottle tops threaded on string

- [ ] castanets — bang two plastic egg cups together

- [ ] tone instruments — tap bottles or porcelain bowls filled with different amounts of water with a metal knitting needle or bamboo stick

- [ ] cymbals — bang two saucepan lids together

- [ ] trumpet — bend a piece of cardboard into a cone shape

- [ ] kazoo — blow on tissue paper wrapped round a comb

SECTION 14

Home Sounds

- ☐ toilet flushing
- ☐ telephone
- ☐ vacuum cleaner
- ☐ washing machine
- ☐ fridge
- ☐ fan heater
- ☐ water running
- ☐ cooking sounds, eg. frying, boiling
- ☐ talking
- ☐ laughter
- ☐ baby crying
- ☐ baby babbling
- ☐ baby burping
- ☐ baby gurgling
- ☐ door bell
- ☐ drill
- ☐ hammer

- ☐ music
- ☐ television
- ☐ radio
- ☐ cassette player
- ☐ music box
- ☐ doors banging
- ☐ door knocker
- ☐ alarm clock
- ☐ crockery chinking
- ☐ footsteps
- ☐ pet noises, eg. barking, mewing
- ☐ cleaning sounds, sweeping, rubbing
- ☐ lawn mower
- ☐ hedge clipper
- ☐ bathing

Human Sounds

- [ ] sighing
- [ ] whispering
- [ ] laughter
- [ ] crying
- [ ] shouting
- [ ] talking
- [ ] voices with different emotions, eg. anger, surprise
- [ ] informal and formal speech, eg. friends chatting, news reader
- [ ] screaming
- [ ] yawning
- [ ] tut-tut
- [ ] oh! mmm! ah! sh!
- [ ] sneezing
- [ ] coughing
- [ ] moan of pain
- [ ] brushing hair
- [ ] washing face or hands
- [ ] cleaning teeth
- [ ] washing hair
- [ ] dressing
- [ ] bathing
- [ ] showering

Section 14: Everyday Sounds & Soundmakers

Everyday
OBJECTS

(!) **Always be extremely careful with small objects which may be swallowed accidentally by young children. Items should be placed in shakers with *secure* lids. If in any doubt, use larger objects or toys. Specialist children's stores, such as Mothercare, sell a device for checking whether objects are small enough to be swallowed.**

☐ safety pins

☐ paper clips

☐ pens or ☐ pencils

☐ keys

☐ coins

☐ tin foil

☐ greaseproof paper

☐ crinkly paper

☐ beads

☐ wooden bricks

☐ sand

☐ *Plasticine*

☐ dried foods

☐ small toys

☐ model vehicles

☐ watch

☐ clock

☐ spoon in cup ☐ in glass

☐ cutlery

☐ spent matches in box

☐ paper strips (use thin cardboard)

☐ pegs

☐ curtain hooks

☐ expanded polystyrene

☐ small stones ☐ pebbles

☐ cotton reels

☐ glasses clinking

☐ books shutting or dropping

☐ scissors cutting paper

☐ pencil being sharpened

☐ water being poured

☐ knife scraping on a plate

☐ watch with electronic bleep

☐ pencil scribbling

☐ fingers tapping on a window or table

☐ door banging

Shakers

You can make your own shakers by collecting everyday objects. Containers can be varied but must have a removable lid and be opaque. It is important that the lid can be placed on the container *securely*: otherwise objects may fly out and cause injury. Any of the following can be used to make a shaker:

☐ jars

☐ plastic camera film containers

☐ plastic storage jars

☐ margarine and yogurt pots

Representational
N O I S E S

- ☐ slide — whee!
- ☐ roundabout — whee!
- ☐ bus — beep-beep; ding-ding; vroom!
- ☐ car — beep-beep; vroom!
- ☐ train — choo-choo; chchch-choo
- ☐ clock — tick-tock
- ☐ telephone — dring-dring
- ☐ cat — miaow!
- ☐ tiger — rarrgh!

P

Animal Noises

Farm

- [ ] cow — moo
- [ ] pig — oink
- [ ] sheep — baa
- [ ] dog — woof-woof
- [ ] cat — miaow
- [ ] cockerel — cock-a-doodle-doo

- [ ] cuckoo — cuckoo
- [ ] chicken — cluck
- [ ] ducks — quack-quack
- [ ] horse — neigh
- [ ] bird — tweet

Zoo

- [ ] elephant — trumpet
- [ ] lion — roar
- [ ] tiger — raargh

- [ ] birds — tweet; whistle; chirp
- [ ] monkey — oo-oo
- [ ] bear — rrr

Pets

- [ ] cat — miaow; purr
- [ ] dog — woof-woof
- [ ] parrot — squawk

- [ ] budgie — tweet; chirp
- [ ] mouse — squeak; eek-eek

Garden animals

- [ ] bee/wasp/fly — bzzzz
- [ ] bird — tweet; chirp

Environmental
SOUNDS

Garden

- ☐ lawn mower
- ☐ birds
- ☐ bees
- ☐ hedges being clipped
- ☐ plants being watered
- ☐ sweeping
- ☐ digging

- ☐ radio
- ☐ people laughing
- ☐ drinks being poured
- ☐ cooking on the barbecue
- ☐ water in a fountain
- ☐ children playing

Street

- ☐ traffic
- ☐ car horns
- ☐ train
- ☐ aeroplane
- ☐ sirens
- ☐ newspaper man
- ☐ road works
- ☐ church bells

- ☐ bus bell
- ☐ car screeching
- ☐ people talking
- ☐ stall holders
- ☐ street entertainers
- ☐ road accident
- ☐ pedestrian signal

Weather

- ☐ wind
- ☐ hailstones

- ☐ rain
- ☐ thunder

P

School

- [ ] intercom
- [ ] bell
- [ ] playground bell
- [ ] whistle
- [ ] chairs scraping
- [ ] chalk on board
- [ ] musical instruments
- [ ] beeps on computer
- [ ] children laughing
- [ ] voice of teacher
- [ ] doors banging
- [ ] windows banging
- [ ] piano

- [ ] singing
- [ ] skipping
- [ ] football
- [ ] children playing, eg. toy bricks dropping
- [ ] dinner plates
- [ ] cutlery
- [ ] playground noises, such as games, skipping songs
- [ ] assembly
- [ ] story time
- [ ] sound of feet

Transport

- [ ] aeroplane
- [ ] train
- [ ] underground train
- [ ] bus, eg. horn, bell
- [ ] car engine

- [ ] car horn
- [ ] motorbike
- [ ] bike bell
- [ ] wheels on a skateboard
- [ ] ship's hooter

Farm

- [ ] tractor
- [ ] animal sounds
- [ ] talking
- [ ] shouting

- [ ] gun firing
- [ ] milk churns
- [ ] lorry
- [ ] cooking

Section 14: Everyday Sounds & Soundmakers

Zoo

- [ ] ice-cream seller
- [ ] crowd sounds
- [ ] animal sounds
- [ ] feeding time, eg. calling to animals, noise of the feeding bucket

- [ ] noise of animals moving or swimming
- [ ] cashier
- [ ] cafeteria
- [ ] souvenir shop

Shops

- [ ] cashier
- [ ] crowd sounds
- [ ] announcements
- [ ] lift, eg. bell-boy, bell to signal doors closing

- [ ] arguments
- [ ] trolley
- [ ] tins falling
- [ ] piped music

Railway station

- [ ] announcements
- [ ] people talking
- [ ] guard
- [ ] flower seller
- [ ] crowd noises

- [ ] buffet bar
- [ ] ticket machine
- [ ] train noises
- [ ] doors slamming

Swimming pool

- [ ] cash register
- [ ] water splashing
- [ ] locker door shutting
- [ ] change machine

- [ ] bell
- [ ] intercom
- [ ] children shouting

Action Sounds

- ☐ clapping
- ☐ stamping
- ☐ dancing
- ☐ skipping
- ☐ rubbing hands together
- ☐ tapping fingers in palm
- ☐ running
- ☐ walking
- ☐ banging

- ☐ clicking fingers
- ☐ hopping
- ☐ tapping toes
- ☐ drumming fingers
- ☐ sliding feet
- ☐ tapping foot
- ☐ knocking
- ☐ jumping

APPENDICES

Further Reading

Cooke J & Williams D, *Working with Children's Language*, Winslow Press/Speechmark Publishing, Bicester, 1988.

Knowles W & Masidlover M, *Derbyshire Language Scheme*, 1979 (contact address: The Area Education Office, Grosvenor Road, Ripley, Derbyshire DE5 3JE).

Lear R, *Play Helps (Toys and Activities for Handicapped Children),* William Heinemann Medical Books Ltd, London, 1977.

Lynch C & Cooper J, *Early Communication Skills*, Winslow Press/Speechmark Publishing, Bicester, 1991.

Newson J & Newson E, *Toys and Playthings*, Penguin Books, Harmondsworth, 1979.

Resources

Musical instruments, soundmakers and other useful materials for listening activities are available from the following.

United Kingdom

Taskmaster
Morris Road
Leicester LE2 6BR
www.taskmasteronline.co.uk

Early Learning Centre
South Marston Park
Swindon SN3 4YJ
www. elc.co.uk
(There are many high street branches around the country.)

Learning Development Aids (LDA)
Abbeygate House
East Road
Cambridge CB1 1DB
www.LDAlearning.com

Speechmark Publishing Ltd
Telford Road
Bicester
Oxon OX26 4LQ
www.speechmark.net

United States of America

Didax Inc
395 Main St
Rowley
MA 01969
www.didaxinc.com

Incentives for Learning
111 Center Avenue
Suite 1
Pacheco
CA 94553
www.incentivesforlearning.com

S & S Worldwide
75 Mill Street
PO Box 513
Colchester
CT 06415
www.ssww.com

The Speech Bin
1965 Twenty-Fifth Avenue
Vero Beach
FL 32960
www.speechbin.com

Super Duper Publications
PO Box 24997
Greenville
SC 29616
www.superduperinc.com

Zany Brainy
3342 Melrose Ave NW
Roanoke
VA 24017
www.zanybrainy.com

Early Skills ... the Complete Series

In dealing with day-to-day management of clients, the Speechmark Early Skills . . . series has established an enviable reputation as the essential resource for every speech and language professional. The following titles are available:

Early Sensory Skills

Jackie Cooke

A compendium of practical and enjoyable activities for vision, touch, taste and smell. Invaluable to anyone working with young children, this text outlines major principles and aims followed by six easy-to-use sections containing basic activities, everyday activities, games and topics to stimulate the senses.

Early Movement Skills

Naomi Benari

This fifth title in Speechmark's *Early Skills* series is designed to help anyone caring for very young children, whether in home, school or clinic. With graded activities, it encourages the use of movement to enhance cognitive, emotional and physical development.

Related Resources

Storycards: Verbs, Prepositions, Adjectives
Sue Duggleby & Ross Duggleby
A new approach to learning basic language concepts.
Social Skills Programmes
Maureen Aarons & Tessa Gittens
An integrated approach from early years to adolescence
Pocket ColorCards®
The world's leading photographic language cards

Early Visual Skills

Diana Williams

This recent addition to the *Early Skills* series is intended for use by professionals who are working with children who have under-developed visual perceptual skills associated with language delay or other communication difficulties. It is a practical manual offering photocopiable activities designed to stimulate and develop visual attention and discrimination skills.

Early Listening Skills

Diana Williams

Early Listening Skills is a highly practical, comprehensive and effective manual for professionals working with pre-school children or the older special needs child. It contains more than 200 activities, all of which can be photocopied.

Early Communication Skills

Charlotte Lynch & Julia Kidd

In this new revised edition of one of the most popular titles in the *Early Skills* series, the authors have updated and revised their educational and therapeutic ideas for work with pre-school children and their families.

These are just a few of the many therapy resources available from Speechmark. A free catalogue will be sent on request. For further information please contact: